The Master's Bouquet and More!

Lorna Sparks Gutierrez

WESTBOW
PRESS®
A DIVISION OF THOMAS NELSON
& ZONDERVAN

Scripture taken from the New King James Version. Copyright © 1979, 1980, 1982
by Thomas Nelson, Inc. Used by permission. All rights reserved.

Scripture taken from the King James Version of the Bible.

Scripture taken from the Holy Bible, NEW INTERNATIONAL VERSION®. Copyright © 1973, 1978,
1984, 2011 by Biblica, Inc. All rights reserved worldwide. Used by permission. NEW INTERNATIONAL
VERSION® and NIV® are registered trademarks of Biblica, Inc. Use of either trademark for
the offering of goods or services requires the prior written consent of Biblica US, Inc.

Scripture quotations taken from the New American Standard Bible®, Copyright © 1960, 1962, 1963, 1968,
1971, 1972, 1973, 1975, 1977, 1995 by The Lockman Foundation. Used by permission. (www.Lockman.org)

WestBow Press books may be ordered through booksellers or by contacting:

WestBow Press
A Division of Thomas Nelson & Zondervan
1663 Liberty Drive
Bloomington, IN 47403
www.westbowpress.com
1 (866) 928-1240

ISBN: 978-1-5127-6115-3 (sc)
ISBN: 978-1-5127-6114-6 (e)

Library of Congress Control Number: 2016917457

Print information available on the last page.

WestBow Press rev. date: 01/20/2017

Dedication

*This book is dedicated to the God of humanity and to those people who wish to serve Christ. I hope it will inspire others to serve Him, and will inspire others to **keep on** serving Him. Thank You, Holy Spirit, for standing by me and inspiring me!*

Foreword

In these poems you will notice that there is an unorthodox play on punctuation, capitalization, and etc. to emphasize certain words, feelings, and rhythms; also, there are commas and dots to emphasize pauses in timing. Too, I did not capitalize the name of satan, as he deserves no glory and is responsible for the world's misery. As far as I know, the devils' fates were sealed the minute Christ died on the cross; and ours was sealed, we who confess Christ, when the Lord arose from the grave.

If you want easy reading for any afternoon or anytime, relax and read these poetic gems to encourage yourself. If you want to know what Christ can do in your life as He has done in mine, then read and believe. If you want to put a smile on your face, then read the family and humorous poems.

*There are many different topics herein which challenge mankind today; I have attempted to address them from a Biblical perspective. With some of the poems you may not agree: (example), "Backward Aborted Society". Remember, in this society it is a matter of choice, even to the point that accepting Christ into your life is **also** a matter of choice; so, feel free to critique! Please know this, Jesus loves you, just as He loves me, and He gave His Life for us all!*

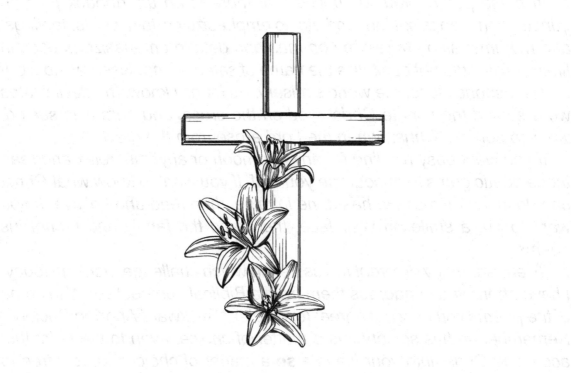

Preface

This book has taken years to unfold: a lot of life's experiences, a great love for God, appreciation for His friendship, and His enduring love for me!

I had asked The Lord for a gift with which I could serve Him, and also to leave a legacy for my children. This book is dedicated to The Lord and what He can do in your life if you truly believe and ask Him!

Please note that the illustrations in this book are in black and white. If this is your book, then please feel free to color them to your heart's desire and with the colors of your choice.

Acknowledgement

The people I have encountered during this life, experiences God has set forth, and inspirations of scriptures have contributed to the material in this book. Without these, there would be no book nor inspirations for writing it. Truly, "…All things work together for good to those who love God, to those who are the called according to His purpose." (Romans 8:28, AKJV).

I want to thank Westbow press for helping me through this publishing experience, and for educating Tisha and I about writing and publishing processes.

I wish to give special recognition to my daughter, Tisha, for helping me type and edit this poetry, and for helping me with researching materials. To my other children, Eugene (his wife, Areli), Brandon (his wife, Evonne), and Dona (her husband, Miguel), I give my thanks for their emotional support for this effort. I also thank you, Lawrence (my husband), for listening to these poems as I wrote them.

Recognition is also given to my sisters and friends in Christ for their inspirations and prayers: Arlene, Kathleen and George, Audrey, Ruth, Barbara, Janis Sue, Katie, Mary and Lee, Louann, Kellie, Elena, Suzanne, Maryanne, Nida, Judi, Lisa, and Sherrie. Also for prayers and encouragement, I'd like to thank my siblings: Betty, Jane, John, and my brother-in-law, Dick; also thanks are to my cousins, Rea and Betty. Thanks are to my grandchildren: Mariah, Ana, Tahni, and Michael for their art-work and help; (and to Joy, Wade, Matthew, and Phoenix Rose for their inspirations also). Recognition is also given to Christian men who have inspired me in their love for the Lord. Thank you all, friends and family!

And to the Greatest of All, Jesus My Lord, Who is definitely my Greatest Inspiration! For those who think I have left out God the Father or the Holy Spirit, remember that They resided in Jesus - the Incarnate Word - the God-Head Bodily. So, Everyone There is included in this body of work!

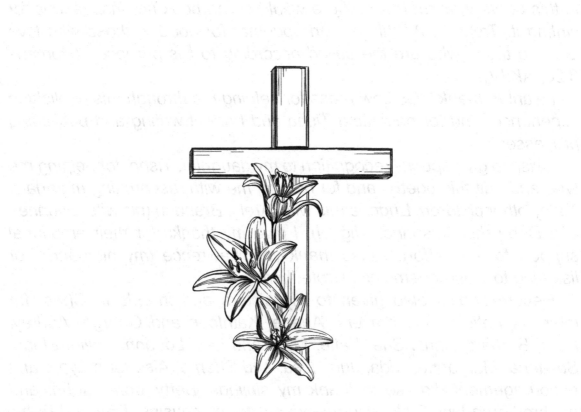

Table of Contents

Religious

And

Ethically

Related

Poetry

A. Religious and Ethically Related Poetry

At Easter Time

They want nothing to do with Jesus,
No more than 2000 years ago.
There is no room in their arrogant hearts,
For selfish pride lives in their souls.

They'd be ashamed to say, "Yes, Jesus is my Lord." --
For their answer to Christ had been - "No".
The costs might be sneers or worldly gain--
It might be life, fortune, or fame.

The same is today as yesterday:
They still stand at Jesus' feet--
As they've hung Him upon the cross in their hearts,
And they wonder why they find no relief!

When He knocks at the door of your heart,
Don't be as the scoffers before!
Is it so hard to say, "Yes, Lord be mine,
And I'll be yours while there's time!"?

One must have an answer for those who ask,
"Why do you believe in the Lord?"
The answer, - "His Spirit bears witness with mine,
And that salvation I can afford!"

The price is free to those who ask.
His love is ever true!
Just simply ask Him, and you'll see--
Salvation's price has been paid for you!
(At Easter Time)

Lorna Sparks Gutierrez

Inspirational Verses
Luke 19:10 (KJV)
10 For the Son of man is come to seek and to save that which was lost.
Romans 8:16,17 (AKJV)
16 The Spirit Itself beareth witness with our spirit, that we are the children of God:
17 And if children, then heirs; ......

Christ, My God!

My ministry for the Lord has been a long, extended one:
To pray for the sick from sunrise to setting sun--
To pray for the broken and bereaved--
To give them hope that they could believe--

That the God I worship, the Risen Christ,
Has come that we might have real life!
He came to lift up the sad and depressed--
To give friendship and peace to those who've wept!

My God isn't made of wood or stone.
He doesn't sit in a grove of trees all alone.
The Lord comes into the hearts of empty men,
And rids them of loneliness, ugliness, and sin!

He came into mine when I was alone.
My sins He forgave - my heart He atoned.
He is real, and His Spirit exists.
You can feel His Presence; That Warmth, you can't resist!

Only the hardest of men with hearts of pride,
Will try to resist and try to hide.
His Spirit can melt even a heart of stone;
So, why should we be weary and all alone?

Now we can have life and hope, anew;
For, Christ came to earth to give Salvation for you!
The Truth will come; just read that Bible so true!
There is New Life - awaiting *you!*

Lorna Sparks Gutierrez

Inspirational Verse
John 10:10 (KJV)
"...........I am come that they might have life, and that they might have it more abundantly."

Christmas In The Heart
(Christ's Mass)

There are those who don't believe in Christmas,
And there are those who do;
And, there are those who believe in the Lord,
As some of us choose, it's true.

Some do not believe - but, this fact must be said:
It's true historic fact Jesus lived, and that He arose from the dead!
Only enlightened spiritual eyes see this, those that are called,
"Born Again".
It's eternal life for those who believe, who desire salvation from sin.

Christmas is simply a mass for the Lord,
A celebration of birth it should be!
(Not really a day for a saint called Claus
Or of exchanging gifts, glittering lights, or jolly glee.)

There's nothing wrong with exchanging gifts,
And nothing wrong with beautiful lights or glee;
But, reality through our thoughts and souls must sift
For what is real and true purity.

If we believe in Christ, let's try this basic perfection:
One day His Nativity, one day His Death, and one day His Resurrection!
To not celebrate His Birth at all, would be something to lose.
So, celebrate His Birthday, whichever day you choose!

And I love the Day the Lord arose - that glorious Day set apart!
To me, more glorious than the glorious three days,
Is the Day Christ arose in my heart!!

That Day of Salvation we should all celebrate;
The Day the Spirit Himself to us imparts!
As ever we should celebrate
CHRISTMAS - IN THE HEART!

Lorna Sparks Gutierrez

Inspirational Verse
Romans 8:16 (NKJV)
The Spirit Himself bears witness with our spirit that we are the children of God.

Matthew 1:18-25 (NKJV)
<u>Christ Born of Mary</u>
18 Now the birth of Jesus Christ was as follows: After His mother Mary was betrothed to Joseph, before they came together, she was found with child of the Holy Spirit. 19 Then Joseph her husband, being a just man, and not wanting to make her a public example, was minded to put her away secretly. 20 But while he thought about these things, behold, an angel of the Lord appeared to him in a dream, saying, "Joseph, son of David, do not be afraid to take to you Mary your wife, for that which is conceived in her is of the Holy Spirit. 21 And she will bring forth a Son, and you shall call His name Jesus, for He will save His people from their sins."
22 So all this was done that it might be fulfilled which was spoken by the Lord through the prophet, saying: 23 "Behold, the virgin shall be with child, and bear a Son, and they shall call His name Immanuel," which is translated, "God with us."
24 Then Joseph, being aroused from sleep, did as the angel of the Lord commanded him and took to him his wife, 25 and did not know her till she had brought forth her firstborn Son. And he called His name Jesus.

Matthew 27:45-56 (NKJV)
<u>The Death of Jesus</u>
45 From noon until three in the afternoon darkness came over all the land. 46 About three in the afternoon Jesus cried out in a loud voice, "Eli, Eli, lama sabachthani?" (which means "My God, my God, why have you forsaken me?").
47 When some of those standing there heard this, they said, "He's calling Elijah."
48 Immediately one of them ran and got a sponge. He filled it with wine vinegar, put it on a staff, and offered it to Jesus to drink. 49 The rest said, "Now leave him alone. Let's see if Elijah comes to save him."
50 And when Jesus had cried out again in a loud voice, he gave up his spirit.
51 At that moment the curtain of the temple was torn in two from top to bottom. The earth shook, the rocks split 52 and the tombs broke open. The bodies of many holy people who had died were raised to life. 53 They came out of the tombs after Jesus' resurrection and went into the holy city and appeared to many people.
54 When the centurion and those with him who were guarding Jesus saw the earthquake and all that had happened, they were terrified, and exclaimed, "Surely he was the Son of God!"
55 Many women were there, watching from a distance. They had followed Jesus from Galilee to care for his needs.
56 Among them were Mary Magdalene, Mary the mother of James and Joseph, and the mother of Zebedee's sons.

Matthew 28:1-20 (NKJV)
<u>He Is Risen</u>
28 Now after the Sabbath, as the first day of the week began to dawn, Mary Magdalene and the other Mary came to see the tomb. 2 And behold, there was a great earthquake; for an angel of the Lord descended from heaven, and came and rolled back the stone from the door, and sat on it. 3 His countenance was like lightning, and his clothing as white as snow. 4 And the guards shook for fear of him, and became like dead men.
5 But the angel answered and said to the women, "Do not be afraid, for I know that you seek Jesus who was crucified. 6 He is not here; for He is risen, as He said. Come, see the place where the Lord lay. 7 And go quickly and tell His disciples that He is risen from the dead, and indeed He is going before you into Galilee; there you will see Him. Behold, I have told you."
8 So they went out quickly from the tomb with fear and great joy, and ran to bring His disciples word.
9 And as they went to tell His disciples, behold, Jesus met them, saying, "Rejoice!" So they came and held Him by the feet and worshiped Him. 10 Then Jesus said to them, "Do not be afraid. Go and tell My brethren to go to Galilee, and there they will see Me."
11 Now while they were going, behold, some of the guard came into the city and reported to the chief priests all the things that had happened. 12 When they had assembled with the elders and consulted together, they gave a large sum of money to the soldiers, 13 saying, "Tell them, 'His disciples came at night and stole Him away while we slept.' 14 And if this comes to the governor's ears, we will appease him and make you secure." 15 So they took the money and did as they were instructed; and this saying is commonly reported among the Jews until this day.
16 Then the eleven disciples went away into Galilee, to the mountain which Jesus had appointed for them. 17 When they saw Him, they worshiped Him; but some doubted.
18 And Jesus came and spoke to them, saying, "All authority has been given to Me in heaven and on earth. 19 Go therefore and make disciples of all the nations, baptizing them in the name of the Father and of the Son and of the Holy Spirit, 20 teaching them to observe all things that I have commanded you; and lo, I am with you always, even to the end of the age." Amen.

Comforting Thought
(For Loss Of A Loved One)

Our hearts are saddened for your loss.
We will pray for God to comfort you
At this time - and always.
The Lord is our only comfort in any situation - Cling to Him.
People run from the Lord, but for those who cling to Him,
He is their comfort!
The Bible says the Lord is the "Lifter of your head".
While we are cast down, He lifts us up.
He said, "He who comes to me, I will in no way cast out!"
Jesus also said, "Learn of Me, for I am meek and lowly,
And you will find rest for your souls."
In these perilous and dreadful times, we need a Savior,
A Friend, and a Comforter!
The Bible says to "Think on these things."

Lorna Sparks Gutierrez

Inspirational Verses
Psalm 3:3 (KJV)
King David said,
"But thou O Lord, art a shield for me: my glory, and the lifter up of mine head."
John 6:37 (KJV)
Jesus said,
"All that the Father gives Me shall come to Me, and him that comes to Me,
I will in no wise (way) cast out."
Matthew 11:28-30 (KJV)
Jesus said,
"Come unto Me, all ye that labor and are heavy laden, and I will give you rest.
Take My yoke upon you, and learn of Me: for I am meek and lowly in heart: and ye shall find rest unto your souls.
For My yoke is easy, and My burden is light."
Philippians 4:8 (KJV)
Saint Paul said,
"Finally, my brethren, whatsoever things are true,.....honest ...just.......pure....lovely....of good report,
if there be any virtue and if there be any praise, THINK ON THESE THINGS."!!!

Cure For Depression

Look to the blessed good that you have done!

For all have made mistakes....except ONE!

And as for God's redemption, then look to Him!

For only Our Redeemer....can forgive us all of sin!

Lorna Sparks Gutierrez

Inspirational Verses
Psalm 3:8 (KJV)
"Salvation belongeth unto the Lord: thy blessing is upon thy people. Selah."
Matthew 9:6 (KJV)
"...But that ye may know that the Son of Man has power upon earth to forgive sins."
Proverbs 12:25 (NKJV), "Anxiety in the heart of a man, causes depression; but a good word makes it (the heart) glad."
(NIV) "Anxiety weighs down the heart, but a kind word cheers it up."

Dear Lord, I'm Thankful!

Forgive me Lord for complaining,
As I have much to be thankful for!
My house may not be as fine as others;
But, thank You for the warm carpet on the floor.

I'm so glad you gave me children.
They've graced my life with love!
Each is precious in his or her own way.
Each was sent to me from Heaven above.

I'll try to raise them as You would have me do;
And, I'll care for the other things You gave me too.
I'll try not to complain, as I should be glad;
For I am blessed for ALL I've had!

Lorna Sparks Gutierrez

Inspirational Verses
Psalm 100: 1-5 (KJV)
Verse 1-"Make a joyful noise unto the Lord, all ye lands."
Verse 2-"Serve the Lord with gladness: come before His presence with singing."
Verse 3-"Know ye that the Lord He is God: it is He that has made us, and not we ourselves:
we are His people, and the sheep of His pasture."
Verse 4-"Enter into His gates with THANKSGIVING, and into His courts with PRAISE. Be THANKFUL unto Him,
and bless His Name."
Verse 5-"For the Lord is good: His mercy is everlasting; and His truth endureth to all generations."

Emptiness To Fulfillment

She walked around the world to find
What could please and satisfy.
But, nothing did! She felt lost; unsettled was her mind.
Satiety, unsatisfied - it seemed nothing to deny!

No smile in her heart - no smile on her face--
For why was she born? What would she do?
Direction for life seemed inane; why run this race?
Who could she ask who cared for her so true?

But, One she forgot - was "He" "old hat"?
Religion? No, but Jesus? Now there! - A little curious of That!
What was He like? How could she find Him about?
She could open the Bible and look to read, en route.

She read in Matthew, Mark, Luke, and John--
Then, decided there might really be "something" there!
Maybe if she'd known Him personally, she'd of Jesus been fond.
But for now, did she dare?

Why not? To know Jesus - personally?!
(Simply, it's one's soul praying down on one's knees).
To speak to Jesus, "Oh, let me know You!"
The Holy Spirit of the Bible is still - and His Word - still true!

To those who come to Him, He will, "in no wise (means) cast out".*
He knows the world cannot truly satisfy - there's no doubt!
Seek Him with all your heart - and you'll find Jesus.
His Spirit will fill you with Love that eternally pleases!

Seek the Lord in the Bible all for yourself.
Don't let another do it for you.
Come to Love's conclusion all by yourself.
Everything else pales in comparison - it's true!

He said if you promised to serve Him,
That nothing good He would withhold from you.
He promises eternal life and peace, "The Forever Friend."
He's my Great Friend - now, how about you?

Lorna Sparks Gutierrez

Inspirational Verse
*John 6:37 (NKJV)
All that the Father gives Me will come to Me, and the one who comes to Me I will by no means cast out.
Deuteronomy 4:29 (NKJV)
But from there you will seek the Lord your God, and you will find Him if you seek Him with all your heart and with all your soul.
Deuteronomy 28:1-14 (Promises of God's blessing on those who obey Him).

Forgiveness: An Easter Message

I asked myself when spurned and hurt,
"What is forgiveness? How does it work?"
I searched for the meaning, I read, I thought--
Christ had said "70x7"; I was sure, more, we ought!

But, it was hard, so hard, to understand or do--
To pass over a sin or transgression, I knew!
A lot of love and compassion, a lot of living, one would do--
Before a person could do it, 'twas probably true!

But Christ could do it! He did IT, you see--
When He gave His life on Calvary's tree!
".....Father, forgive them, for they know not what they do!"*
Were Christ's intelligent words, and very, very true!

We think we're right, when we may be wrong.
Our ancient ideas may be really foregone!
To be like Christ would be more wise--
Then true wisdom we'd have - and not that surmise!

Can you or I pass over a transgression or sin?
Only if love is bigger can both our hearts mend.
The Only Love I know that is real, is Jesus'!
He demonstrated that by the Spirit He would leave us!

That Spirit is the Holy Spirit of God's Christ!
The Spirit that gives us Rest, gives us Life!
God help me to forgive as You forgave me,
By showing Your Love on Calvary's Tree!

Lorna Sparks Gutierrez

Inspirational Verses
* Luke 23:34 (NKJV)
Then Jesus said, "Father, forgive them; for they know not what they do."
Matthew 6:14 (NKJV)
Jesus said, "For if ye forgive men their trespasses, your heavenly Father will also forgive you."
Matthew 18:21-22 (NKJV)
*Then came Peter to Him, and said, "Lord, how oft shall my brother sin against me, and I forgive him,
till seven times?"*
22:Jesus saith unto him, "I say not unto thee, 'Until seven times': but, 'Until SEVENTY times SEVEN'." !!!
Matthew 11:29 "......learn of me......and you shall find rest unto your souls!"

Giving

By giving a gift you'll keep it--
In your heart forever it stays.
By giving you've multiplied it--
As the sun gives away its rays!

Lorna Sparks Gutierrez

Inspirational Verse
Luke 6:38 (KJV)
Jesus said, "Give, and it will be given to you; good measure, pressed down, and shaken together, and running over, shall men give into your bosom. For with the same measure that you mete* withal it shall be measured to you again."

*Mete-to give out or distribute

How To Become A Christian

Is it so hard to become a Christian?
How does one do it?
Well, sir!--Now listen!

First, I saw I needed God.
I needed and wanted to belong to Him--
That in my present condition,
I needed forgiveness of sin!
Then, I told God that I wanted to be His child--
That I no longer wanted to be wicked or wild!

Suddenly, a miracle happened!
The Gift of Salvation was mine!
The indwelling of The Holy Spirit,
Well, was Truly Divine!
And…. was baptism so hard?
No, it was just easy as could be!

It's pretty deep - this Bible Book!
And in Its reading, I had taken a good look.
Some are afraid to open Its cover--
Some Scriptures may be confusing,
As some would discover!

Now I'm a bit older of a Christian.
As in quiet to The Holy Spirit,
His voice I did listen!
The confusion became less,
As His Spirit made me to understand
More of man's beginning, more of his end!

Because I took Christ by the hand,
He buried my sins for all eternity!
This opportunity is open for you and for me.

So, how is it to be a Christian?
I'm very happy! Oh, please listen!
For, now I'm His and I have the Lord.
Daily, we walk together in one accord!

Lorna Sparks Gutierrez

Inspirational Verse
John 3:6-7 (KJV)
Jesus said, "That which is born of the flesh is flesh; and that which is born of the Spirit is Spirit."!
"Marvel not that I say unto thee, 'Ye must be born again'."

In Honor Of My Aunt Verna
(Her words in reference to the Bible)

Oh, may these Heavenly Pages be
My ever, dear Delight!
And still, new Beauties may I see,
And still, increasing Light!

In Honor of Verna Norton Jameson

Jesus Loves You!

Jesus loves you - Yes, He does--
Surely as there are stars above*******!

Eyes that see and ears that hear,
Cannot fathom all God's years.

All we understand and know
Is nothing next to God, and so--

God can take what little we have, and He can make
A miracle of beauty from even a mistake!

He'll take our weaknesses and make us strong--
Because Jesus, our Redeemer - doesn't do it wrong!

Just trust Him daily; His Love is all ours.
Jesus gives us strength to get thru these hours.

Yes, Jesus loves you - Yes, He does--
Surely as there are stars above*******!

Lorna Sparks Gutierrez

Inspirational Verses
Nehemiah 8:10 (KJV)
"...........for the JOY of the LORD is your STRENGTH."!
1 John 4:8 (KJV)
".........for GOD is LOVE."!

Jesus' Name #1

The man began to curse arrogantly; he wanted others to hear him apparently!
His words caught my attention, as The Lord's Name he did mention.

Anger ripped my heart for a moment - but prayer quieted my soul,
As this age old sin reared its ugly head so bold!

Personally, I felt his ignorance and his arrogance.
Spiritually, my eyes could see the devil gleefully dance!

It shocked me somewhat, as I suppose was his point.
I didn't know exactly what to say, except to ask Christ's Spirit on me to anoint.

I could feel the Lord's Spirit, That Precious "Jesus My Lord".
I felt like rejoicing for I could feel our Spirits in one accord.

So, I prayed to God for that man, that Jesus would talk to his heart--
That the inspiration of the devil, old satan's influence, would now depart.

I asked God to speak to him, to give him wisdom and knowledge.
At times we need those gifts from the Lord - even those who've "gone to college".

I know they don't know Jesus - those, who don't respect His Name--
That's because they've never met Him - but, blasphemy's sin all the same!

If you see someone sin, pray for him and remember, pray for me too--
For, erring is ignorance and sin - as all of us seem to do!

But Please! If you meet Jesus Christ, remember to honor His Name!
For Jesus is Wonderfully Precious you'll find - His Spirit lives up to His Fame!

Lorna Sparks Gutierrez

Inspirational Verse
Deuteronomy 5:11 (KJV)
God said to Moses--"Thou shalt not take the name of the Lord thy God in vain: for the Lord will not hold him guiltless that takes His name in vain."

Jesus' Name #2

I had just passed by as I heard her say
The Name of the Lord in an inappropriate way!
Did she not believe that Christ heard her words profane?
For God said, "I'll not hold him guiltless who uses My Name in vain!"

Did it make her popular with her friends to use a cliché' so worn,
That made no sense to her, for someone's God to scorn?

Oh, Jesus Christ? Is He here too?
Well, I hope so, my dear!
Don't be a fool, but wise --
For, God has ears to hear!

And, best you know for you shall find
That once you speak His Name,
That He expects the addressing of a prayer--
And not His Name profaned!

The next time you say, "Jesus Christ",
Continue with what should be in your heart.
It could be the beginning of a Friendship,
With a Friend who will not depart!

Lorna Sparks Gutierrez

Inspirational Verses
Exodus 20:7 (NKJV)
7 "You shall not take the name of the Lord your God in vain, for the Lord will not hold him guiltless who takes His name in vain."
Psalm 139:20 (NKJV)
20 For they speak against You wickedly;
Your enemies take Your name in vain.
Acts 22:16 (NKJV)
16 And now why are you waiting? Arise and be baptized, and wash away your sins, calling on the Name of the Lord.

Judging Aright

Be not so swift to judge,
For just one error does not evil a person make!
And, do not so swiftly hold a grudge,
For no one having lived,
Has been devoid of a mistake!

God sees to the heart,
Even to the inner core.
Another cannot peer there--
Not even to enter that door!

Only God holds the key to the heart!
Only He can judge so swift!
Only He knocks, can enter, and see so smart.
Only God can judge - only He has THAT gift!

We must pray for wisdom,
If we are to discern aright.
If we all listen to God's Voice,
We'll keep peace between us in sight.

Then peace will enter in,
As sin can then no longer reign!--
Thankfully, there will be no choice for
God's great WISDOM to obtain!

Lorna Sparks Gutierrez

Inspirational Verses
Matthew 7:1-2 (KJV)
Jesus said,
1. "Judge not that ye be not judged. 2. for with what judgment ye judge, ye shall be judged: and with what measure ye mete, it shall be measured to you again."

18

Little Feet

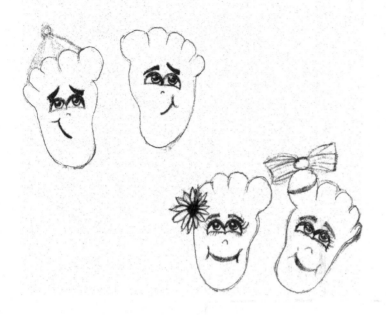

Little Feet

Your demeanor and your actions may be okay to you.
And, you might even excuse yourself for just a wrong or two.

But Little Feet don't know it; THEY think that ALL is right!
So be so VERY careful how you walk tonight!

Little Feet might just follow exactly where you go;
They'll even try to walk BETTER than your 'fast or slow'!

Little Feet will mimic all you do and say!
So watch WHERE and HOW you walk;
Remember, some "Little Feet" may be admiring you today!

Lorna Sparks Gutierrez

Inspirational Verse
Matthew 18:6 (NKJV)
"Whoever causes one of these little ones who believe in Me to sin, it would be better for him if a millstone were hung around his neck and he were drowned in the depths of the sea."

"La-Rue"

"Guero"

"Winkies"

"Mouse"

"Silent Night"

4's LORNA "Magestic Night"

Mom,
tea,
Book

Majestic Night

As I had sat down to rest and pause,
I was not thinking of Santa Claus--
But, of the children, who lay at my feet.
Near the bright tree, they were fast asleep!

Surely they were dreaming of Christmassy things,
Of treasured gifts, and all that gleams!
I felt the beauty the tree exuded,
Decored* with lights and shiny cuties*******!

Warm tea near my hand, a book nearby--
With gratefulness, a tear fell from my eye.
I thought of Baby Jesus,
And how He slept His First Night--
And how the Angels kept Him,
As His Stars did shine so bright*******!

Lying in a manger, so meek, so mild,
Was Christ Jesus, our Savior - a God-and-Human Child!
His sleep was Holy, and it seemed,
That He dreamt the dreams that babies do dream!

So tomorrow, little children, when you awake,
There is Another Gift for any man to take!
For many years ago, the Christ-Child was born.
His Gift? - That our sins He would atone!

NOW, and every Christmas, there is FREE,
The Gift of Salvation, for YOU and ME!
There wouldn't be a Christmas,
Except for His Sacrifice!
So thank You Lord, in remembrance,
On This Majestic Night!

And tomorrow, when we all awake,
The Choice is ours - God's *GIFT* to take!

Lorna Sparks Gutierrez

Inspirational Verses are the first 2 chapters of the books of Matthew and Luke of the New Testament.
(Please read these and enjoy)

Decored: Just another poetic word for decorated!

Note: Jesus, Himself, is the Gift of Salvation!
He gave Himself for the Atonement of our sins!

My Song Unto The Lord

My soul doth pant after Thee, Oh Lord,
To claim that prize of Thy Reward--

Of Love, and Peace, and Serene Calm--
To please Thee - from dusk thru dawn!

My soul doth in Thee to hide
From life's stress and satan's ugly guide.

Save unto Thee to look, all else is gone!
In Thee, my Heart - my Soul - my Song

Shall ever be of Thee, Oh Lord,
To sing Thy Song in One Accord!

Lorna Sparks Gutierrez

Nine Gifts Of The Spirit

"But the manifestation of the Spirit is given to every man to profit withal".*
These gifts are given to us to enable us to stand, for us not to fall.

There is only one Spirit, but there are nine gifts.
These are given to His saints for bonding of the church,
And not given for rifts!

The 1st is the Word of Wisdom--to make us wise.

The 2nd is the Word of Knowledge--love it; do not it despise!

The 3rd is Faith--too much of it we lack.

The 4th is Gifts of Healing--to break the satanic attack!

The 5th is the Work of Miracles--it really does exist.

The 6th is Prophecy--don't let your ears resist!

The 7th is Discerning of Spirits--we know of whom they are.

The 8th is Diverse Kinds of Tongues--to serve Christ near and far!

The 9th is Interpretation of these Tongues--
The Spirit opens the understanding of some.
In recognition of these, many converts have been won!

Some are given to all, and all are given to a few
For Christ's Works here on earth--for the Spirit to do!

Lorna Sparks Gutierrez

Inspirational Verses
*1 Corinthians 12:1-11
New King James Version (NKJV)
Spiritual Gifts: Unity in Diversity
1 Now concerning spiritual gifts, brethren, I do not want you to be ignorant: 2 You know that you were Gentiles, carried away to these dumb idols, however you were led. 3 Therefore I make known to you that no one speaking by the Spirit of God calls Jesus accursed, and no one can say that Jesus is Lord except by the Holy Spirit.
4 There are diversities of gifts, but the same Spirit. 5 There are differences of ministries, but the same Lord. 6 And there are diversities of activities, but it is the same God who works all in all. 7 But the manifestation of the Spirit is given to each one for the profit of all: 8 for to one is given the word of wisdom through the Spirit, to another the word of knowledge through the same Spirit, 9 to another faith by the same Spirit, to another gifts of healings by the same Spirit, 10 to another the working of miracles, to another prophecy, to another discerning of spirits, to another different kinds of tongues, to another the interpretation of tongues. 11 But one and the same Spirit works all these things, distributing to each one individually as He wills.

"Only God"

We can converse until we're blue in the face.
We can talk until it's simply a disgrace!
But as for some, only God can them persuade...
We can try, tho' it seems our efforts are at times, mislaid!

Without God's Spirit as our Spiritual Guide,
Left by ourselves, to others, we to them only chide!
But, the Holy Spirit convinces as only HE can!
Our part is just to obey and to pray, dear man!

We, His instruments, must His Truth portray.
The rest is left to God, His message to relay.
Remember His glory is His alone!
We must humbly bow before His Glorious Throne!

So, today if someone is convinced or saved,
You simply obeyed and obediently prayed.
Remember Jesus' Spirit brought it to be!
For "ONLY GOD"-------allows one "to see"!

Lorna Sparks Gutierrez

Inspirational Verse
Romans 8:16 (KJV)
"The Spirit Itself beareth witness with our spirit, that we ARE the Children of God."!

Our Backward Aborted Society

We think we are so intelligent.
We think we are so smart.
Our society has to be the most Civilized.
We are now 'State of the Art'!

But let me tell you something...
We are no more civilized than a million years ago!
We also pass our children through the 'Fire'
To sacrifice to 'gods of long ago'!
I can remember reading about them.
They put their babes on the altar!
And bowing to a god unseen,
They cut the child asunder!

Don't we do the same - and give it a medical name?
Bowing to the 'god of convenience'
And the 'god of medicine',
Isn't it really just the same?

That society of years ago will rise up
And judge us soon,
When the Creator calls us home
At morning, night, or noon!
For the Creator told us not to kill babes.
He told THAT society too!
But, we are no better at obeying than
Unlearned, uncivilized loons!!

Now, shall we take the children
To give them to a heathen god?
Or raise them heathenish for "him"?
'Twill be the same old odd!

I see many children walking around unloved.
It breaks my heart anew
To see they were unloved before they were born,
And unloved afterwards too!
I'd rather be a Christian or compassionate,
And keep that poor little child.
I know God would want me to love him
For just a little while!

Realizing there are questions and answers
Even the government can't come up with,
Other than obedience to Jehovah God,
Judgment of mine may not be so swift.
Transporting is an answer - to give the child away;
Whether in utero or after birth,
There are people who would GLADLY take the child today!

But, it's food for thought - so eat it when you can!
Are we REALLY so civilized,
So thoroughly modern man???

Lorna Sparks Gutierrez

27

Our Backward Aborted Society
Inspirational Verses

Jeremiah 32:35
New King James Version (NKJV)
35 And they built the high places of Baal which are in the Valley of the Son of Hinnom, to cause their sons and their daughters to pass through the fire to *Molech, which I did not command them, nor did it come into My mind that they should do this abomination, to cause Judah to sin.'

Psalm 127:3 (NKJV)
3 Behold, children are a heritage from the Lord,
The fruit of the womb is a reward.

Exodus 20:13 (NKJV)
13 "You shall not murder."

Exodus 20:2-3 (NKJV)
2 "I am the Lord your God, who brought you out of the land of Egypt, out of the house of bondage."
3 "You shall have no other gods before Me."

Psalm 106:37-48 (NKJV)
37 They even sacrificed their sons and their daughters to demons,
38 And shed innocent blood, the blood of their sons and daughters,
Whom they sacrificed to the idols of Canaan;
And the land was polluted with blood.
39 Thus they were defiled by their own works,
And played the harlot by their own deeds.
40 Therefore the wrath of the Lord was kindled against His people,
So that He abhorred His own inheritance.
41 And He gave them into the hand of the Gentiles,
And those who hated them ruled over them.
42 Their enemies also oppressed them,
And they were brought into subjection under their hand.
43 Many times He delivered them;
But they rebelled in their counsel,
And were brought low for their iniquity.
44 Nevertheless He regarded their affliction,
When He heard their cry;
45 And for their sake He remembered His covenant,
And relented according to the multitude of His mercies.
46 He also made them to be pitied
By all those who carried them away captive.
47 Save us, O Lord our God,
And gather us from among the Gentiles,
To give thanks to Your holy name,
To triumph in Your praise.
48 Blessed be the Lord God of Israel
From everlasting to everlasting!
And let all the people say, "Amen!"

(cont'd on next page)

Our Backward Aborted Society
Inspirational Verses Cont'd

Leviticus 20:4-5 (NKJV)
4 And if the people of the land should in any way hide their eyes from the man, when he gives some of his descendants to Molech, and they do not kill him, 5 then I will set My face against that man and against his family; and I will cut him off from his people, and all who prostitute themselves with him to commit harlotry with *Molech.

Psalm 139:13-18 (NKJV)
13 For You formed my inward parts;
You covered me in my mother's womb.
14 I will praise You, for I am fearfully and wonderfully made.
Marvelous are Your works,
And that my soul knows very well.
15 My frame was not hidden from You,
When I was made in secret,
And skillfully wrought in the lowest parts of the earth.
16 Your eyes saw my substance, being yet unformed.
And in Your book they all were written,
The days fashioned for me,
When as yet there were none of them.
17 How precious also are Your thoughts to me, O God!
How great is the sum of them!
18 If I should count them, they would be more in number than the sand;
When I awake, I am still with You.

Who is Molech?

According to the Old Testament, Ba'al Molech was one of the heathen gods to which people in ignorance and disobedience would sacrifice their children.

Our Lives Do Matter

Our lives are but little dots...........
Upon the map of time!
As depression, stress, and trouble start,
We forget to plan - for we begin to whine!

That our lives do matter, we mustn't forget!
And the past, our best we did, we mustn't regret.
Just plan, don't fret, and do one's best.
Life, expected or unexpected, will do the rest.

Keep a cheery countenance and give yourself a space.
Life's joys will embrace you as a dress designed with lace.
For, it's the little joys that make this life so real--
That attach to the heart - 'tis so good to feel.

You cannot yield to sorrows, nor on them stand, but step.
Look not back too much on them with weighty regret.
For sorrows will come, and sorrows will go;
They stretch us, and stir us, and cause us to grow.

*As Paul said in Christ, "Overcome, but be not overcome."
And, it takes more than just one's own strength, lest one succumb.
I found that when my strength was low and my soul so tattered,
That giving my life to Christ was the difference that mattered!

Lorna Sparks Gutierrez

Inspirational Verses
Matthew 11:28-30 (KJV)
"Come unto me, all ye that labor and are heavy laden, and I will give you rest. Take my yoke upon you, and learn of me; for I am meek and lowly in heart: and ye shall find rest unto your souls, For my yoke is easy, and my burden is light."
John 16:33 (KJV)
"These things I have spoken unto you, that in me ye might have peace, in the world ye shall have tribulation: but be of good cheer; I have overcome the world."
Nehemiah 8:10 (KJV)
"....Do not sorrow, for the Joy of the Lord is your strength."
(St. Paul's words) Romans 12:21 (KJV)
"Be not overcome of evil, but overcome evil with good."

Our Total Destiny

The manner in which we speak
Can make us strong or weak.

We can build our self respect
By keeping strong emotions in check.

The way in which we see
Decides our opinions and destiny.

The wisest choice, to see your side and mine,
The results of decisions should then be refined.

The way in which we hear
Could make us angry or have us endear.

If we can hear with wisdom, bridling the emotional,
Our reactions would then not hold consequences unmentionable.

The way in which we think
Will make us rise in every way or sink.

*'Tis said, "What we think is what we are."
It grows to be true, we find, so far.

The way in which we do
Will be remembered forever true!

Our endeavors, our actions, and reactions will tell
Our future, our present - if we have risen or fell.

The way in we choose
Determines whether we win or lose.

All things summed together, our senses demand our best--
If we ever intend to conquer ourselves on Life's great adventurous Quest!

Lorna Sparks Gutierrez

Inspirational Verses:
Please read The Book of Proverbs
*Proverbs 23:7 "For as he thinketh in his heart, so is he."

Peace With The Lord

Is quiet, confirmed, reserved.
In quietness of the soul is
A joy refined,
A blessing unfurled,
A gift Divine!

To feel His Presence,
To bow in awe,
To reach His Outstretched Arms,
To be One in Soul,

To rest assured in
An "EVER" Friend,
To know this <u>real</u> Communion *is*
A Love without end!

Lorna Sparks Gutierrez

Inspirational Verse
Jeremiah 29:13 (KJV)
"And ye shall seek Me, and find Me, when ye shall search for Me with all your heart."

Praise Jesus

Oh forgive Lord, the secret sins of my heart.
Forgive the froward way my heart tends to follow.
I praise You for bringing my heart back into line--
For leading my heart onto a straight path--
For lifting my heart onto higher ground--
For filling me with joy and laughter!
Praise the Name of the Most High God!
Praise the Name of the Lord Jesus!
Christ the Lord be praised - be magnified!
Be lifted high up <u>forever!</u>

Lorna Sparks Gutierrez

Praising God In Prayer!

In praising God is true ecstatic delight,
Joy of the soul in swelling flight!

Majesty of His Spirit falling down upon you,
Will make you know His Love is *true!*

In truly seeking Christ with all your heart,
You'll find His Love is real...and not just in part.

There is wholeness and healing of body and soul
Of one who really seeks God so bold!

The Heat of His Spirit from your head to your toes,
Fills you from top to bottom, and delights your soul!

Prayer is more than asking; it's communion with God.
As man seeks His Creator, he finds Oneness with God.

Know Rest that exists, as the Apostle Paul said.
Know Jesus Christ, the Spirit of The Lord, from your foot to your head!

That Holy Spirit is of Christ, the Divine Love of Jesus!
My spirit rests in His, with Love that Eternally pleases!

Lorna Sparks Gutierrez

Inspirational Verse
Deuteronomy 4:29 (KJV)
"But if from thence thou shalt seek the Lord thy God, thou shalt find Him, if thou seek Him with all thy heart and with all thy soul."

Priorities - Christ Speaks

Are you alone? You feel you've no friend?
Do you see nothing in life's obscure end?
Are you confused? Is your heart in pain?
Does life seem that it's all in vain?

(PRIORITIES)
Now...be honest with yourself - did you really try the Lord?
Did you give Jesus your heart or just the part you could afford?
You mustn't put Him last; you have to put Him first,
Just as you should have done, when you received the NEW BIRTH.

Now I hear you say, "I went to church and tried the Lord.
Then Jesus let me down; I lost all that I adored!
Death took my child; I lost my best friend.
Jesus didn't answer my prayer; so, that's all - the end!"

(CHRIST SPEAKS)
"Now child, hear Me, you must love Me best!
You'll find your strength in Me - the Joy of the Lord, your Rest.
I too loved your child - before you, he was Mine.*
And in answer to your prayer, 'twas,
'Not now, 'tis not the time'."

"Just trust Me again - I can help you with your life.
Prayer can ease your pain - give me your hurt, your strife.
Your child and friend await you - they await with Me.
I can give you the Peace of Christ for all eternity!"

"So come back unto Me - Be Mine once more.
Open up your heart - I knock at the door.
The priorities will align - faith will enter again.
Life is yours anew--
For, I have the Power to forgive sin!"

Lorna Sparks Gutierrez

Inspirational Verses
Luke 20:38 (KJV)
*Jesus said, "For He is not a God of the dead, but of the living: for all live unto Him."
Isaiah 40:31 (KJV)
"But they that wait upon the Lord shall renew their strength; they shall mount up with wings as eagles;
they shall run, and not be weary; and they shall walk, and not faint."
Psalm 27:14 (KJV)
"Wait on the Lord: be of good courage, and He shall strengthen thine heart:
WAIT, I SAY, ON THE LORD." !!!
Nehemiah 8:10 ".....for the Joy of the Lord is your strength!"

Remember to Pray

When your heart is weary,
When your soul is sad,
Remember, Someone Somewhere loves you.
Remember and be glad!

When your heart is weary,
And your brow is furled,
Remember the Rest that Christ can give.
Do you remember that He overcame the world?

When your heart is weary,
Don't forget to PRAY---
The Spirit of God can lighten the countenance.
Remember, His Presence shows you the Way!

For, when your heart is happy,
Remember, it once was not.
And remember, for it was in PRAYER,
The answer that you sought!

Lorna Sparks Gutierrez

Inspiration Verses
1 Thessalonians 5:17 and verse 24 (KJV)
note: please read the verses in between, they are good also!
(17) Pray without ceasing.
(24) Faithful is He that calleth you, Who also will do it !
Philippians 1:6 (AKJV) St. Paul said:
"Being confident of this very thing, that He which hath begun a good work in you will perform it until the day of Jesus Christ:"

Speaking In Tongues

I was a skeptic and had not believed
Of those, 'twas said, who spoke in 'tongues'.
Although the Bible said it was true that some had received,
Others told me it had been just for those Apostolic ones.

So, I took what others had said for gospel,
Yet my heart fought me for that place.
I could not rest - for the subject was hostile.
So, I set the Bible before me to search in haste.

I prayed o'er the subject in fear and disbelief.
Yet I knew I had to accept the Bible or not!
And, the God who inspired those words was Chief;
So, I humbled myself as in prayer the answer I sought.

I believed in my heart - but was it for me?
Oh yes, God answered. He did. How grand!
For, one night I awoke and found myself praying
In a language only God could understand.
My hand on his heart and the other lifted up,
And in words I did not comprehend,
Somehow my soul knew, and God did too,
The prayer that was prayed for that lost man.

Now, I had to believe, for that was God's way to show me,
To not criticize what I did not understand.
For all is not conscious, and all is not seen,
And all is not fully understood, dear man!

However, God is All in All, a Spirit Unseen,
So ever Glorious and All Inspiring still!
He can speak to us in many different ways,
To manifest Himself as He will!

The Spirit one can feel, and I've heard Him call my name.
Yes, His voice can truly be heard!
Oh, life can be grand when lived with such a Man,
As Christ the King, the Incarnate Word!

So believe Him, friend, what He says - He can do!
If you let Him, He can even speak through you!
He said in John 7:38 and 39, of that Holy Spirit
And the Living Waters you will find.

The Lord has said His Spirit is yours for the asking.*
See Acts 10:46 and 11:16 of Holy Ghost baptism--
See Romans 11 verse 29, God is not sorry for His gifts so fine--
For those who believe not, tongues are but for a sign. **

Just trust the Lord - let His Spirit flow in you.
Give Him your heart - nothing less will do!
Hear the Lord's voice - allow the Lord to live in your being.
Keep humble before Him - see with His Seeing.
You will be amazed at the miracles sublime--
And hold dear to your heart, Holy Words heard divine!
Trust the Lord now for Spirit Gifts at your New Birth,
And, truly know the Pearl of Great Price - a Treasure of Immeasurable Worth! ***

Lorna Sparks Gutierrez

Luke 11:13(AKJV) "......How much more shall your Heavenly Father give the Holy Spirit to them that ask Him?"
**In reference to 1 Corinthians chapter 14:22; chapter 14 is explanatory.*
***Matthew 13:45-46 (AKJV) (45) "Again, the Kingdom of Heaven is like unto a merchant man, seeking goodly pearls: (46) Who, when he had found One Pearl of Great Price, went and sold all that he had, and bought it."*
Note: Jesus paid the "Great Price" for our entrance into the Kingdom of Heaven! Jesus is synonymous to the Kingdom of Heaven to me. Wherever He is, is where I want to be! And He is more than a Precious Pearl to me!

The Eunuch

Not visibly born male nor female, but still of His worth.
The third sex? No! Only human creatures of God,
Perhaps deformed at birth.
Society tries to make them fit - by surgically altering them.
That's great, IF it's okay, but not to accept them as they are, is sin.

We need to accept those who are not like us.
If someone's a little different - so - what's the fuss?
Some can be helped - perhaps others cannot.
There's no one upon which to lay blame or fault.

*Some are Eunuchs by birth, some by men, and some by accidents.
God has given men medical knowledge to
help these - setting precedents.
Those who want peace of mind, their bodies may be changed.
And, others who have peace of mind, they
may choose to stay the same.

Eunuchs are people with minds and souls like you and me.
For, it is the soul that really counts, you see!
Jesus came down to save us ALL on this Earth.
For, His Promise is to ALL, the Gift of Jesus' Worth!

Lorna Sparks Gutierrez

Inspirational Verses
Galatians 3:28(KJV)
"There is neither Jew nor Greek, there is neither bond nor free, there is NEITHER MALE NOR FEMALE: for ye are all ONE in Christ Jesus!

Isaiah 56:3-5 (KJV)
3) ...Neither let the Eunuchs say, "I am a dry tree!"
4) For thus saith the Lord unto the Eunuchs that keep my Sabbaths and choose the things that please me, and take hold of my covenant;
5) even unto them will I give in My house and within My walls a place and a name BETTER than of sons and of daughters: I will give them an EVERLASTING name, that shall not be cut off.

*Matthew 19:12 (Jesus' Words) (KJV)
12) "For there are some Eunuchs which were so born from their mother's wombs and there are some Eunuchs which were made Eunuchs of men and there be Eunuchs, which have made themselves Eunuchs for the Kingdom of Heaven's sake. He that is able to receive it, let him receive it."

The Face Of Jesus

I've heard it said, "Do others see Jesus in you?"
And then I read - to "Follow the Steps of Jesus.", too!
Consequently, when a homeless soul I see,
Mixed emotions churn inside of me.

Some work - others are not able.
Some try - others are not mentally stable.
So what do we do - and try not to feel like a fool?!

Well for once, does he not feel foolish too?
What has reduced the wretched soul to such ado?
Surely he is not proud to beg for food.
And, I'd be ashamed if I were rude!

These people need a program to help them get on their feet.
The rest of us need to gather to think
Of something smart and something neat:
A program that will help them to help themselves and others--
A program that is fair to ourselves - and to our downcast brothers!

*The Lord said, "I was naked, and you clothed me not;
I was hungry, and you gave me no food;
I was thirsty, and you gave me no drink."
So now brother, don't you agree we need to think?

We're responsible to each other in our own way,
To do what Christ said for us to do each day!
I don't have the answer - not by myself!
Except, it won't really cost me much to give of my wealth!

So, of what are you afraid, people? What are the reasons?
What will you say when you see the face of Jesus?
If I can see the face of Jesus in them,
Will they be able to see the face of Jesus in you and me?
God help us to please Him and not to sin.
Let us follow the Lord's Steps and be more like Him!

Lorna Sparks Gutierrez

Inspirational Verses
Matthew 25:42 (KJV)*
Jesus said, "For I was an hungered, and ye gave me no meat; I was thirsty, and ye gave me no drink."
Matthew 25:40 (KJV)
"And the King shall answer and say unto them, 'Verily, I say unto you, Inasmuch as ye have done it unto one of the least of these my brethren, ye have done it unto Me'."

The Future

Taking one day at a time,
And that day's goals,
With long range plans in mind,
Daily, the future unfolds.

With Faith as your partner,
And Surety as your guide,
The plans of the heart
Are opened wide!

For, as we also have plans,
So does the Lord!--
Plans for a future full of peace, of hope--
As daily we live and try to cope.

The Lord wants to be your Guide,
As daily, challenges bring.
For it is His good pleasure
To see your soul's heart sing!

Lorna Sparks Gutierrez

Inspirational Verse
Jeremiah 29:11 (KJV)
"For I know the thoughts that I think toward you, saith the Lord, thoughts of peace and not evil, to give you a future and a hope."

The Master's Bouquet

As God was in His Garden Eden alone,
The beautiful flowers He planted had grown:
Reds, greens, yellows and blues - so bright and fair--
Grew lovingly, stately, and gracefully there.
God looked upon them and saw how lovely they were,
And He was pleased with His endeavor's allure!
"Why not adapt this idea to other plans?" He thought--
"I'm lonely here on this earth's Eden plot."
So, He made His Adam and then His Eve.
Then, He sculpted others in creativity He perceived:
Reds, browns, ebony, yellows, whites, even varied crèmes--
His human bouquet was unique - He deemed!
Statures He built: muscular, tall, slim and square.
His ideas even expanded to the eyes and the hair:
Blondes, browns, blacks, and reds varied;
Eyes of greens, turquoises, browns and blues,
Rare violets, grays, golds, and even blacks, He dared!
How proud He was of His creation,
Encompassing colors of every nation!
However, it seemed one day to His displeasure,
The humans He'd gifted with minds of great measure,
Had dared to defy Him by judging each other!
"How dare them", God thought--
"I want them to be brothers!"
Just as the flowers grew together by the way,
He wanted His people to get along well each day!
So, God left them over to reprobate minds;
Each was seeking after his own peculiar kind.
Many years passed, and man sinned against man,
Finding fault with each other - out of God's plan!
So, God devised a New Plan - It was Christ!
And all who looked upon Him could have New Life!
For the Spirit of Christ has NO color you know--
No form but that of God, Spirit, and Soul!
If we are to ever overcome secular leaven,
Our souls must become the Color of the Christ of Heaven!
Then, we can all fit into Christ's bouquet,
To be beautiful in His Garden as He intended that day!
We can be most happy and never alone--
We'll be beautiful in His Color,
His blood has for us atoned!
Let us now of Heavenly wisdom partake,
And this earthly kingdom willingly remake.
We can enjoy living on this earthly sod
--By seeing each other with the Eyes of God!--

Lorna Sparks Gutierrez

The Master's Bouquet Inspirational Verses

Inspirational Verses

The History of Creation and Man
Please read Genesis, Chapters 1 & 2 of The Old Testament in the Bible

The Rebellion of Mankind
Please read Romans, Chapters 1 & 2 of The New Testament in the Bible

Jesus, the New Covenant
New King James Version (NKJV)
Hebrews 12:24-27 to Jesus the Mediator of the new covenant and to the blood of sprinkling that speaks better things than that of Abel.
25 See that you do not refuse Him who speaks. For if they did not escape who refused Him who spoke on earth, much more shall we not escape if we turn away from Him who speaks from heaven, 26 whose voice then shook the earth; but now He has promised, saying, "Yet once more I shake not only the earth, but also heaven. 27 Now this, "Yet once more," indicates the removal of those things that are being shaken, as of things that are made, that the things which cannot be shaken may remain.

That God is a Spirit
John 4:24 (AKJV)
(Jesus said)
24 "God is a Spirit: and they that worship Him must worship Him in spirit and in truth."
John 6:63 (NKJV)
(Jesus said)
63 "It is the Spirit who gives life; the flesh profits nothing. The words that I speak to you are spirit, and they are life."

The Miracle of Salvation through Christ
2 Timothy 3:15 (NKJV)
And that from childhood you have known the Holy Scriptures, which are able to make you wise for salvation through faith which is in Christ Jesus.
1 Thessalonians 5:9 (NKJV)
For God did not appoint us to wrath, but to obtain salvation through our Lord Jesus Christ,
John 3:1-8 (NKJV)
1 There was a man of the Pharisees named Nicodemus, a ruler of the Jews. 2 This man came to Jesus by night and said to Him, "Rabbi, we know that You are a teacher come from God; for no one can do these signs that You do unless God is with him."
3 Jesus answered and said to him, "Most assuredly, I say to you, unless one is born again, he cannot see the kingdom of God."
4 Nicodemus said to Him, "How can a man be born when he is old? Can he enter a second time into his mother's womb and be born?"
5 Jesus answered, "Most assuredly, I say to you, unless one is born of water and the Spirit, he cannot enter the kingdom of God. 6 That which is born of the flesh is flesh, and that which is born of the Spirit is spirit. 7 Do not marvel that I said to you, 'You must be born again.' 8 The wind blows where it wishes, and you hear the sound of it, but cannot tell where it comes from and where it goes. So is everyone who is born of the Spirit."
John 3:16-17 (NKJV)
16 For God so loved the world that He gave His only begotten Son, that whoever believes in Him should not perish but have everlasting life. 17 For God did not send His Son into the world to condemn the world, but that the world through Him might be saved.
John 10:7-11 (NKJV)
7 Then Jesus said to them again, "Most assuredly, I say to you, I am the door of the sheep. 8 All who ever came before Me are thieves and robbers, but the sheep did not hear them. 9 I am the door. If anyone enters by Me, he will be saved, and will go in and out and find pasture. 10 The thief does not come except to steal, and to kill, and to destroy. I have come that they may have life, and that they may have it more abundantly.
11 I am the good shepherd. The good shepherd gives His life for the sheep."

The Three in One

I think I slightly understand…because that I am ME,
That God is 3 in 1 and also 1 in 3!
He isn't like us; however, we are somewhat like He.
That is why He sent Jesus, so we could more plainly of Him to see!

Some people say, "Why do you believe there are 3, when there is only 1?"
It is that the Godhead is fulfilled in Jesus, God's only begotten Son.*
In Isaiah, God said, that He was the Redeemer; that beside Him there was no other.
And, that His Glory He would not give to another.

HOWEVER, He said that He would send HIS SALVATION (as the One in Isaiah 53):
The PROMISE of the Holy One, the Lamb of God, a Messiah.
Jesus confirmed it as He read in Isaiah chapter 61,
It tells of Christ's Coming, the Entrance of the Son!

Jesus read from Isaiah; see Luke 4 and verse 18.
And in John 14:9, "whosoever has seen Me, there has also the Father, been seen"!**
In Isaiah 44:6, He said He was the King of the Jews;
And Pilate left those words on the Cross in super inscription too!

He is the Word Incarnate, see John chapter 1.
Verse 14 says "…made flesh, and dwelt among us…" - That Holy One!
Is it so hard to understand how God can be God and still, Man?
But He is God: Omnipotent, Omnipresent, and Omniscient - hard to understand?

His Flesh cried to His Spirit on Calvary.
He knew the pain He'd go through for you and me.
God is a Spirit - there is only
"One". ***
He did Great Works thru God Incarnate, the Son!

The Holy Ghost conceived Jesus, see Luke 1, and verse 35.
The Holy Ghost is also the Comforter that Jesus sent to help us survive!
The Father, the Holy Ghost (the Comforter, the Holy Spirit), Jesus (The Word),
They are God All the Same,
And All are thru Jesus - now just one Name! ****

Is it hard for us to understand? - We only see as Man--
How God is Omnipotent, Omnipresent, Omniscient - In the Universe and in the hearts of Man.
Humble yourselves and simply believe that Jesus is God's Lamb.
Jesus said In John 13:13, "Ye call me Master and Lord, and so I AM"

Well, that is ENOUGH proof for me, fellow Christian man!
The more I've read, I've found more in the Bible.
But read it for yourself - have a PERSONAL Revival!

Lorna Sparks Gutierrez

Inspirational Verses
*Colossians 2:9 (KJV)
9 For in Him (Jesus) dwelleth all the Fullness of the Godhead bodily.
**John 14:9 (AKJV) Jesus said to Philip, "….he that hath seen Me, hath SEEN the Father"!
***1John 5:7 (AKJV) St. Paul said, "For there are three that bear record in heaven, the Father, the Word, and the Holy Ghost: and these three are one.
Ephesians 4:4 (AKJV) St. Paul said," There is one body and one Spirit, even as ye are called in one hope of your calling;"
Note: the Holy Ghost, the Holy Spirit, the Comforter - are the same and these names are used inter-changeably in the Bible. Jesus Christ was referred to as "The Word, who was made flesh and dwelt among us", as in John 1: verses 1-14.
****Zechariah 14:9 (NASB) and the Lord shall be King over all the earth: in that day there shall be One Lord and His Name, The Only One.
Note: NASB is the New American Standard Bible-AKJV is the Authorized King James Version.
Also read 1 Corinthians 8:6, Isaiah 52:10, 13-15, and Isaiah 53:1-12.
Don't worry if you may be confused if you are human – He is God, and He will take care of it all!

True Ethical Reasoning

If you stand up and say, "All is OK, and is not sin!",
And do not discern between righteousness and wrong,
And base your beliefs upon equality ONLY,
And not base them upon GOD,

Then, you will put your relationship with God in jeopardy.
It would be as far-distanced as before you were saved!
Rethink as you REREAD that Bible--
Either you believe it or NOT (those ideas are rival!)

Reread the Bible; believe It is Truth - It has stood the Test of Time!
Work out your own salvation with trembling and fear,
And know that God speaks His truth; lend your spiritual ear!

As you read that Bible Book to work out your own salvation,
You will learn God's truth, validating spiritual revelations!
Faith-belief-trust: it takes all three to seek God's truth eternally.
Prayer, searching, and discernment is really just
To grow in God's truth, these are a MUST!

Fearing is a Respect to Him of Whom we believe.
Knowing He is not weary, His Blessing we do receive!
Holy Respect and Honor is in His Name!
What He has SACRIFICED for us, we will not profane!

Love and pray for others
Who refuse to listen or to believe;
For, REALLY ALL you want for them,
Are Jesus' promises to receive!

Lorna Sparks Gutierrez

Inspirational Verses
Philippians 2:12 (NKJV)
Therefore, my beloved, as you have always obeyed, not as in my presence only, but now much more in my absence, work out your own salvation with fear and trembling;
John 5:39 (NKJV)
39 You search the Scriptures, for in them you think you have eternal life; and these are they which testify of Me.
James 5:16 (NKJV)
Confess your trespasses to one another, and pray for one another, that you may be healed. The effective, fervent prayer of a righteous man avails much.
John 8:32 (NKJV)
32 And you shall know the truth, and the truth shall make you free.
Isaiah 17:7 (NKJV)
In that day a man will look to his Maker, And his eyes will have respect for the Holy One of Israel.
1 Chronicles 16:10-11 (NKJV)
10 Glory ye in his holy name: let the heart of them rejoice that seek the Lord.
11 Seek the Lord and his strength, seek his face continually.
1 Chronicles 16:34 (NKJV)
34 Oh, give thanks to the Lord, for He is good! For His mercy endures forever.
John 14:6 (NKJV)-Jesus said, "I am the Way, the Truth and the Life…………"
Also, read (NKJV) the 1st. chapter of Romans- God did state in Malachi 3:6- "I am the Lord, I change NOT." So, work out YOUR own salvation with fear and trembling; and trust what Paul said in Philippians 1:6- "that He, who begun a good work in YOU, will perform it until the day of Christ Jesus." That will put faith in you, and your heart will rest a bit better.

What And Who Is God?
(For Children or Anyone)

God is the Creator of the worlds.
He made you, me, and other boys and girls.
God is The Great One of the universe.
He's the One we worship when we go to church.

God wasn't happy with the ways of Man.
So, God had thought up for us a New and Better Plan:
That on the First Christmas, Jesus Christ would be born,
To be our Savior and Redeemer, on THAT glorious morn!

Since God is a Spirit, His Spirit lived in Jesus.
He called Him His Son to show us what God is!
Jesus died on a cross so we wouldn't have eternal strife.
So, if we would believe on Him, we would have Eternal Life!

God loved us so much that He sent His only Son.
That New Plan is in action; Eternal Life has now begun!
All you have to do is believe in God--
Believe He loves you and cares for us all!

Accept His New Plan, Jesus: THAT Plan has begun.
And you will be called ONE of His ones!
Eternal Life is yours; accept Him now!
And IT will happen - The Holy Spirit knows how!

Jesus' way is easy; His burden is not hard.
He's our Friend, our Helper, and our Light in the dark!
He'll always be yours if you ask Him to be.
The promise of Salvation is for you and me!

Jesus is the best Friend that I've ever had!
If you accept Him.....You will be glad!

Lorna Sparks Gutierrez

Inspirational Verse
Matthew 18:3 (NKJV)
And (Jesus) said, "Assuredly, I say unto you, unless you are converted and become as little children, you will by no means enter the kingdom of heaven."

Wine Bottles and Garment Cloths

A new theory, a new thought, a new way,
Into an "old" mind-set cannot be!
No more to teach an old dog new tricks--
Only Christ could do it masterly!

The only way it could be done,
The "old" mind, it had to be renewed!
The new ideas could then settle in,
And new thoughts could then ensue.

'Tis said in the Bible, one cannot put
A new garment piece upon the old;
Nor put new wine into old bottles,
They would rend – they would burst; I was told!

Christ won't come into the "old mind-set" man,
He comes only into a new!
For that is what salvation is!
That's what it <u>does</u> for me and for you!

The "old mind-set" man doesn't want the Lord,
And doesn't desire His ways;
But the touch of the Master's hand,
Has a way of changing those ugly nights to bright new days!

Christ can come into your old heart,
And He can make you brand new!
But, only if you want it;
The choice is yours - that Gift of Salvation true!

So, you can't like the new wine*,
Until your "old bottle" is renewed;
And that's only by the Master's Hand!
His miracle of Salvation, it's just for you!

The "old" garment, that's torn and hurt,
Cannot be renewed with just a new piece.
The old has to be wholly discarded and replaced.
It's so easy to find "NEW" Spiritual Release! **

Just ASK Jesus to come into your heart;
<u>Repent of those "old ways" to accept His New!</u>
By His Miracle of Salvation, you'll see a New Heart,
*New 'Wine', **New 'Garments', and .....
New Life - Too!

Lorna Sparks Gutierrez

Inspiration verses
Matthew 9: 16-17 (KJV)
16. No man putteth a piece of new cloth unto an old garment, for that which is put in to fill it up taketh from the garment, and the rent is made worse. 17. Neither do men put new wine into old bottles: else the bottles break, and the wine runneth out, and the bottles perish: but they put new wine into new bottles, and both are preserved.
Note: In the Bible, in Communion, wine is symbolic of the blood of Christ.*
Read Matthew 26:28.(NKJV), "For this is My blood of the New Covenant, which is shed for many for the remission of sins." Therefore, wine symbolically, in the New Testament Communion, represents - the blood of Christ, which purifies us of sin.
***Isaiah 61:10 "I will greatly rejoice in the Lord, my soul shall be joyful in my God; For, He has clothed me with the garments** of Salvation, He has covered me with the robe of Righteousness......."*

Your Book of Life

My mother told me that for me, there was a Book of Life another could read.
And that Each of Us has one; in ours, daily the angels write
Of the good and bad we do daily - of our wrongs and our rights.

I surely hoped the Lord had an Eraser that could change the pages there!
I hoped the pages would later read of better choices much more fair.
I learned there was an Eraser, that JESUS was His Name!
And, He could take those bad choices, thereby changing this Life's Game!

The Changing was called Forgiveness; For, Jesus had a better Plan!
And, if I followed in His Footsteps, I could be a happy man.
To fall in love with the Master Writer was all one had to do.
Only He had the Gift of Salvation, where one could write his own book so true.

One's life is but a book for another soul to read.
Another will see mistakes made there, and in wisdom he should take heed.
He will also see there, good done; he'll see happiness - he'll see pain.
And, one should read there quietly to garner wisdom's gain.

I also say respectfully; for each person has
A story to tell, both happy or sad.
No one, you know, can walk in another's steps
To judge there much, for another's steps to tread.

For some souls are weak and others are strong.
Right to one, to another is wrong!
Some decisions made, another would have changed;
They believe their outcome would not have been profaned!

Perhaps they are right, perhaps not so.
Only the Lord in His Wisdom for sure would know.
And, certainly in this Life we should all take heed.
For, Each of Us has a Book for another to read!

Lorna Sparks Gutierrez

Inspirational Verse

Psalms 139:16 (NKJV).......And in Your Book they all were written, the days fashioned for me, when as yet there were none of them.

Poetry

To

Encourage

B. Poetry to Encourage

A Blessing For You

May your joys be many--
May your sorrows be few--
May the Light of the Son
Dawn upon you!

Just as the morning sun
Kisses the welcome dew,
May blessings jump to run--
May they shower over you!

Lorna Sparks Gutierrez

A Little Spark Of Light

We are all given a "little spark".
One just needs to find the niche--
Ours, to lighten any dark
To cause the demons to flee and flinch!

A little spark may light the way
Of another, stumbling in dubious dark,
To deter one who may otherwise sway--
"Flee torturous demons - and then depart!"

Oh, see the value of groping souls,
Their hope of just one light!
Others see, to take heart and note
To live in ecstatic hope and might!

Let not others your hope take,
But give One Hope to them --
That the Light of Christ will not forsake
Those who look to Him!

Lorna Sparks Gutierrez

Inspirational Verse
Hebrews 13:5 (KJV)
".....I will never leave thee, nor will I forsake thee."

A Man's Life

A man's beginnings may be humble.
His start in life may be strife.
Abuse may cause him to stumble,
And curse the existence of his life.

Hunger and cold may assault him.
Despair may seem life's goal.
He may feel that hope is slim,
And loneliness might fill his soul.

Hey, dear brother, don't be adread!
There really IS a Friend out there.
He is the One who had no place to lay His Head.
His Life with you, He is willing to share!

He can provide friendship and warmth from the cold,
And provide a place to lay your head--
Enough love to fill both body and soul--
"To live life more abundantly", He said.

Just whisper His Name and call out to Him.
"Ask and receive", He said.
"Prove me herewith", He said to them.
His Spirit is Alive, He is NOT dead!

Just tell Him your heartaches and pain.
He has the salve to soothe the soul,
With feelings of love that remain.
His Spirit is Alive - you see!
His Salvation will last for ALL eternity!

I've found His promises to be true - Hold on and don't let go!
Tell Him you need Him and want Him - He's here!
All He asks is your heart and your soul!

He's loving and kind and will do you no wrong.
He'll cause your heart to sing a new song.
He is the ONE who wants to please us.
My dear friend, call Him....His name is Jesus!

He has advice that's sound and sure;
And for any ill, He is the Power to cure.
Truly, He has a will for your life and mine.
Daily, He wants you to live a life more fine!

Lorna Sparks Gutierrez

Inspirational Verse
John 10:10 (KJV)
Jesus said, ".........I am come that they might have life, and that they might have it more abundantly."

A Parent's Golden Rule

Not everyone has a good mother
That they can brag about.
Nor does everyone have a good dad,
Of that there is no doubt!

However, not every parent has a good child!
Some are sort of civilized,
And others are sort of wild!

I think that the point comes down to caring--
For both the child and the parent.
Caring is loving - both are sharing--
Whether, if you be obedient or you be errant!

Parents and children can make this world better
By seeking their Maker's will and not to deter!
One can avoid a daily duel
By simply living….that Golden Rule!*

Lorna Sparks Gutierrez

*The Golden Rule:

Inspirational Verse
Matthew 7:12 (AKJV)
Authorized King James Version
"Therefore all things whatsoever ye would that men should do to you, do ye even so to them: for this is the Law and the Prophets."

A Poem Of You

To a lively and vibrant spirit,
(Whose star is not shining so bright)
This note is sent to cheer it,
So it can twinkle******* once more with delight!

There are visions out there to conquer,
And friends you haven't yet met.
So Mon Cheri, do not languor!
Life has just begun - it is not over yet!

Open your heart and mind to adventures!
Let Love and Life flow anew!
Be likened to Love,
And Life, do not censure!

Then soon loved ones will see
A Merry, Sprightly, New YOU!

Lorna Sparks Gutierrez

A Prayer Of Praise

Oh Lord, My God,
That I love You so!
And that, I want the world to know.

Sometimes I'm weak and easily fall.
Except for You, I'd be nothing at all!

But You make everything real to me!
You create in me, mold, and reshape me
To make me more like Thee!

Then, I become more of what You desire:
More of Your creation - more entire!

More of You lives in me each day.
It looks better as You model my clay.

Thank You for Your Spirit, Your love, Your beauty,
Your freedom, Your thought, and reward of duty!

Thank You for life! Thank You for You!
May this world know You…… even MORE than I do!

Lorna Sparks Gutierrez

A Thought On Death

Before they go, the worst we fear,
The loss of ones we love so dear!
We ache, we hurt, we strive, we pray
For God to heal - to answer right away!
The slithering thoughts through our minds behold
What hereafter must be like - we are only told!

For them we fear the unknown that they face!--
And, for us who are left - deepest desolateness!
This, a part of life, we must also enter--
Not alone - as all of us seek solace from
Some wise, unembittered mentor.

For peace we seek and hope we must,
Else our life is over before our destiny is thrust.
Let us join together in loving and sharing,
Making our lives much better by each measure of caring!

Then, the worst we fear, even death, cannot threat;
Because our faith with our works,
Will overcome for us yet!

Lorna Sparks Gutierrez

....And Heaven's Family Garden

The Lord has a garden in Heaven; He plants it one-by-one.
Then, He gives a piece of the garden to each family as it's done.
Each person is a seed of God's garden, planted on the soil of the Earth,
*Designed by the Master Creator, determined before time of birth.

We are all His children - old and young alike!
Our purpose is above our knowledge: in His knowledge, in His Light!
We must humbly bow before Him - even when we don't agree
As to how and when He plants that garden - be it beast, or you, or me!
We are like that garden - like the seeds and seedlings fair.
Some will grow upon the Earth - and others in His Kingdom there.

Eventually we all stand before the Master Creator
To determine where we will best fit.
And, it hurts when we are transplanted, because on Earth
We see His Plan only bit-by-bit!
We will never understand it all, except in the bye-and-bye--
When God reveals to us His Master Plan,
And, Its beauty - *revealed* - to the naked eye!

Our true home is in Heaven; Earth is just - but a start.
In Heaven's garden we'll see our family,
Those now gone, yet still, left in our hearts!
And, in Heaven it shall be revealed to us
**As to how we fit into the Grand Design;
For, we are only 'taken' to be there replanted—
***Note: We, our spirits, shall NOT be left behind!

By: Lorna Sparks Gutierrez

Inspirational Verses

Psalm 139: 13,15,16 (NKJV) 13 "For you formed my inward parts.......15 Your eyes saw my substance, being yet unformed. 16 And in Your book they all were written, the days fashioned for me, when as yet there were none of them."!!!

**1 Corinthians 2:9 (NKJV) But as it is written, "Eye has not seen, nor ear heard, nor have entered into the heart of man, the things which God has prepared for those who love Him."!!!*

***Hebrews 13:5 (NKJV).......for He Himself has said, "I will never leave you nor forsake you."!!!*

A Weak Moment

I'll assess, my strength can be small--
Even my wisdom - sometimes not at all!
But, there are times I'm strong and bright.
I even help others to see the light!

Tho while I am weak, I should not badly feel--
When I can thank God that His Love is real!
To remember blessings from the past - these I recall;
And in hope I look forward better - to feeling enthralled.

Lorna Sparks Gutierrez

All Is Well

All is well if I should die.
For really, really, what care I?
Except to see my loved ones well,
To see them in peace and in safety to dwell!

But as for me, I have Christ the Lord!
My heart is His in one accord.
And, in Heaven I'll fly in God's fair sky--
So, all is well if I should die!

Lorna Sparks Gutierrez

An Ode to a Mother and Child

An Ode To A Mother And Child

She was young, hungry for love, and unwise.
She gave herself to a man, full of charm and guise!
How many of us have been like her? Too many we know!
Youth has its trust, and abuse makes us bitter. - So,

She told him they were going to have a baby.
What would they do? Would he marry her maybe?
Oh, he'd see about it - "Not to worry, Hon!" - He had to go.
But then, he never came back with an answer! - So,

Eventually, she couldn't hide it anymore; she told her mother.
Mother told father, and since he was "old-fashioned", Oh brother!
Dad turned his head; she was no longer his daughter. - Well, she had to go!
And mom stood by dad; she had shamed them too much - So,

She packed her bags and left in a cold wind, crying.
Where could she go? She walked on thinking, sighing!
A man stopped his car, and took her to a police station.
She needed information, you know.
Someone gave her the address of a girl's home - So,

She got a ride - hitched a few until she got there.
They befriended her, and counseled her rightly and fair!
Eventually, she had a pretty baby girl; she saw her - Oh!
Dried the tear in her eye, kissed her longingly bye. - So,

She got a job with friends' help, and came into her "own".
After years of work and prayer, she finally forgave her folks
Of the opportunity they had blown:
To help their child thru troubles and sorrows--
And, get them on to better tomorrows! - So,

If she'd had the chance to keep her baby,
They might have been together - maybe!
But, life turned its chance, and they found each other!
All those tears in her heart turned to joy for daughter and mother! So,

Although they weren't as yet "mom and daughter", but new-found friends,
They shared life-times of stories, and marveled at "the end"!
Bad things don't have to stay bad, and lemons don't have to stay sour!
The good comes if we wait, work, and pray - we'll see that desired hour! So,

Ask the Lord - Who works miracles, where else none would abound!
He picks us up - sets our feet on higher ground!
He takes our bad and turns us all aright,
By the Power of His Spirit, His Friendship and Might!

Lorna Sparks Gutierrez

An Overdose In Bed 3
(An ER Experience)

I was amazed - but not so much - to her answer, "Go away!"
She didn't obviously want the answer to her ills.
So, why did she take that overdose of pills?
Did she want attention, or really to die?
I thought it over, and I wondered why.
"Twenty or so", her neighbor had said she'd taken.
That woman in bed 3 was past being shaken!
She threw up charcoal on my pants' leg.
Sighing, I hoped her lifestyle didn't also include AIDS!
We were next to her in the ER, a curtain between us.
The care was quite procedural, not much of a fuss.
I was glad to know she'd make it just fine.
But, the rest would be up to her down the line.
The nurse questioned, "Had she been depressed?"
A cry emerged from her, and then digressed.
I tried to comfort her; I said, "I'll pray for you.
God can help ANY problem....it's true!"
That made her wake up even more as she said, "Go away!"
Quietly, I turned and shut the curtained door.
Then, I wondered when we moan and groan with problems sore,
When Christ knocks on our hearts to speak,
Do we also shut the door?
I knew He was the answer for her problems - as well as mine.
Only with the Lord's help, those answers she'd find!
Then, I spoke quietly for God to give her the Light--
To show her that path in life she could sight.
For I knew how well Christ's Light can shine--
That He would be hers as well as mine!
I could go away and still for her, to pray--
As I wondered at the impact that was made that day.
The answer isn't in an overdose of pills;
For Christ is ALWAYS the answer for spiritual ills!

Lorna Sparks Gutierrez

Angels For A Season

An Angel flew down from Heaven
To embrace us for a Season.
When he flew back to embrace the Lord,
We wondered why....the reason?!

It makes us think of knowledge,
That as on earth we roam,
That some people perhaps are angels,
And Heaven's our real home!

We'll see those Angels stand with us,
Beholding the Glory of the Lord--
As we cross that Great Divide,
And enter Heaven's Door.

Lorna Sparks Gutierrez

Are We Much Offended?

Are we much offended?
Too much?
Just smile - it's just a filling of the cup!

Be not much offended at little slights.
The offender may be ill, or some misled a mite.

Just smile, be gentle, and yet firmly stand
To kindly let them know - you're a "man"!

You can handle this situation, this little strife--
As there are small ones and big ones in this complex life.

Are you much offended?
Ah, now be cool!
Live a little by that Golden Rule!

Put yourself in another person's place.
In an act of kindness, arrange a smile on your face.

Offended? I'll try not to be!
It's so much easier to live.....happily!

Lorna Sparks Gutierrez

Inspirational Verse
Luke 6:31 (KJV)
"And as you would that men should do to you, do ye also to them likewise".

Being Older

I am, I know,
Older now.
The patina of youth
Has gone from my brow!
Wrinkles and age spots
Appear from nowhere.
And, I use lotions and creams
Now more than I care!
My teeth are looser,
My eyes more dim,
And too, I hope others don't see me so well!
Should I muster a grin? ☺
I don't run so fast;
My senses have eroded.
My figure is larger;
It looks nearly exploded! "O"
But I guess I can do;
I see others like me!
But, it holds small comfort
That misery loves company!
Now, I shan't put me on a shelf.
Please just love me
In spite of myself!
I still have, you see,
Lots and lots to give.
And, lots of good years
I hope to live!
Everyone you see
That lives, will age.
Just hold fast to a sense of humor;
And, be a bit of a sage!

Lorna Sparks Gutierrez

Inspiration Verses
Psalms 92:14 (NKJV)
"They shall still bear fruit in old age...."
Isaiah 46:4 (NKJV)
"Even to your old age, I am He. And even to grey hairs will I carry you. I have made, and I will bear; even I will carry, and will deliver you."

Thank You, Lord!

Believing God And His Word

As you read the Bible, you must know this truth:
It has proved the test of time; It has never been unproved!
And, as you attempt to read Its pages with avid intrigue,
Pray the Holy Spirit will open windows of knowledge to lead.

To respect His Person, is to reverence His knowledge.
For His creative ability, He did not have to go to college!
So for this, when we read, we need to be in awe.
And, we need to believe it, for we based His wisdom in our laws!

Fearing is a respect to Him of Whom we believe.
Knowing He is not a liar*, His blessings we do receive!
Holy respect and honor is in His Name.
What He has sacrificed for us, we will not profane!

Love and pray for others who refuse to believe.
For you want for them also, Jesus' promises to receive!
As you read the Bible Book, to work out your own salvation,
God's truth will be revealed to you - validating spiritual revelations!

Faith, belief, and trust: it takes all three--
To seek God's truth for all eternity.
Prayer, searching, discernment, respect, and trust--
To grow in God's truth - these are a MUST!

You will find the answers to all of life's questions.
His Spirit will reveal them; Ask and receive - for His Directions.
Remember, to receive Him and His Invitation, it is your choice.
And, in the Bible pages - the Scriptures - you will hear His Voice!

Lorna Sparks Gutierrez

Inspirational Verses

John 5:39 (NKJV)
Jesus said:
"Search the scriptures, for in them ye think ye have eternal life, and they are they which testify of Me."

*Titus 1:2 (NKJV)
St. Paul said:
"...in hope of eternal life which God, who cannot lie, promised before time began...,"

John 10:27 (NKJV)
Jesus said:
"My sheep hear My voice, and I know them, and they follow Me."

Better Thoughts

Rich in thought or poor in thought,
Are we ever what we ought?
What can we do or can we say
To make others feel 'tis better today?

Strive not with each other, but for the goal:
That life will be greater as new days unfold.
The past is lost; the present, contain.
From the past....only wisdom should remain.

Regret not what is gone, but make today the best.
For, all things come and go, or else we'd have no rest!
And, no matter what we've loved or leased,
It shan't be just what we crave.
For we, as humans, are never pleased;
Or else, we'd quit to rant and rave!

There is wisdom… in accepting ourselves quietly.
And, hope that change will be for the better rightly.
Patience with ourselves and others we hope to achieve;
In so doing, some unfathomable, dark burden will be relieved!
And anyway, I'll look to tomorrow and be grateful for today--
While looking for greater achievements with God
In thought, word, and deed for this mortal clay!

Lorna Sparks Gutierrez

Bull By The Horns

Take the bull by the horns.
Do not let him go!--
Lest he throw you high,
And you land back in thorns!

The same way with Life--
Don't wilt like the flower!
Face off with its strife--
Do it hour by hour!

Then rest in knowledge
That you fought the fight
And won!
You did it! You did!
What HAD to be done!

Lorna Sparks Gutierrez

Inspirational Verses
Proverbs both chapters 6 and 24 (KJV)
Also Proverbs 12:24
"The hand of the diligent shall bear rule: but the slothful shall be under tribute."

Depression: A SOLUTION

It's the devil's business you know,
To make you feel so bad you can hardly go!
You look at the world through dim faded glasses--
Life has you sour; dreams fade; all are 'alas-es'!

Stop! Smell the flowers - Bend an eye to them!
Look at their color closely - See the beauteous ascent!
Observe, as the sun comes up, a flower opens its beauty;
And as dark descends, the flower closes in duty.

Now remember, that flower is as the same as your soul;
When one takes his eyes off the Son, he loses his goal!
Keep your eyes on the Light; He'll guide your day.
The Brightness of Love will guide your way.

Don't keep in the dark - the devil wants you there!
That enemy desires you to stay in depression and despair!
Pray and ask God to show you His Light--
That Jesus will guide your steps, and give you His strength in the night!

Remember with Christ in you, you are never alone!
His Glory is bright - He sits on God's throne!
So push depression, the devil, and sadness away--
Walk hand-in-hand with Christ Jesus, The Light of the Day!

Lorna Sparks Gutierrez

Inspirational Verses
Philippians 4:13 (KJV)
Saint Paul said, "I can do all things through Christ who strengthens me."
Matthew 7:8 (KJV)
Jesus said, "For every one that asks receives........."
Note: This whole chapter of Matthew is great, so read it all for full enjoyment!

Each Person Has A Reason

God has given each one a talent--
(He has left no one out!)
Talent with which to serve Him--
And talent to make another man take thought.

Even a man who cannot think or move,
Can inspire another man to think to move;
And perhaps to improve on his own work,
Should perhaps, he must it to prove!

--So, every man is for something, be one rich or poor--
And, God can bless that any man can be more--
By prayer that is answered and work in accord,
Any man should reach his goals....and final rewards!

Lorna Sparks Gutierrez

Inspirational Verse

Luke 1:37 (KJV)
"For with God nothing shall be impossible."

Enthusiasm

Be Glad! Be Happy! Get Excited!

Just think of ALL you have in which you can be delighted!

Just for one moment - what would
happen were they blotted out?

Then ALL your joy you'd lose with a sorrowful shout!

So, Be Glad! Be Happy! Get Excited!

Just think of ALL you have in which you can be delighted!

Lorna Sparks Gutierrez

Inspirational Verse

Nehemiah 8:10 (KJV)
".......the joy of the Lord is your strength."

Exiting Obscurity

Into the depths of darkness
My soul walks.
Onto rocky paths and crevices steep,
I climb slowly,
Cautiously, examining the deep!

Preparing a clear path for others to follow,
Lest they fall beside it and be lost,
I light the way and hold their hands--
And count the costs!

Lorna Sparks Gutierrez

Inspiration Verse

Isaiah 60:19 (KJV)
"..........but the Lord shall be unto thee an Everlasting Light, and thy God thy Glory."

For The Lonely Woman

I waited upon him for all hours of the night.
I waited and waited until morning light.
His covert expression told me that he'd lied.
My heart inside me, in part, somehow died.

But now he is gone - however, I'm not alone.
A Spirit of Love is with me - my heart, the Spirit's throne.*
I don't have to wait upon Him for all hours of the night.
The Love is here to guide me; the Spirit's Love is Bright.

A man might forsake me and leave me alone;
But, God's Love is Forever - Love to me He has shown!
He can show that Love to you; seek it and you'll find
A Love ever so Grand - that gives one Peace of Mind!

Lorna Sparks Gutierrez

Inspirational Verses
Jeremiah 29:13 (NKJV)
"And you will seek Me and FIND Me, when you search for Me with all your heart."
Isaiah 54: verse 6(AKJV)
For the Lord hath called thee as a WOMAN forsaken and grieved in spirit, and a wife of youth, when thou wast refused, Saith thy God.
Isaiah 54: 4-5
Fear not; for thou shalt not be ashamed; neither be thou confounded; for thou shalt NOT be put to shame: for thou shalt forget the shame of thy youth, and shalt not remember the reproach of thy widowhood any more.
(5) For thy Maker is thine husband; the Lord of Hosts is His Name; and thy Redeemer the Holy One of Israel; The God of the whole earth shall He be called.
Verse 13 is excellent: And ALL thy children shall be taught of the Lord; and great shall be the peace of thy children!

*Is the Holy Spirit sitting on the throne of your heart?
Woman, thy Maker is thy Husband! What a Wonderful and Faithful Man, our Great Redeemer! Indeed, God is Love!

In His Father's Eyes

Love streams forth from the Heart thru the eyes,
To build confidence in the soul of a tiny life.

That love is reflected in the eyes of the soul,
As life goes on - and the cycle unfolds.

A Father's Day present one can surmise,
Is that any child is reflected in His Father's Eyes!

Lorna Sparks Gutierrez

Inspirational Verse
Ephesians 6:4 (KJV)
St. Paul said:
"And ye fathers, provoke not your children to wrath:
But bring them up in the nurture and admonition of the Lord."
P.S.
The Lord is Our Good Father!
We are His children!

Jesus, Our Friend

Oh, where are my companions?
They have strung me here and there.
When once - I was there to love them--
And now - where are they to care?

I shared my thoughts and moments.
I was lonely, as were they--
Or so I thought, as they left me--
Now all that's left me - is to pray!

I'll just consult my Dear Friend!
He's always there for me!
Even if awhile I had left Him,
He would, once more, re-welcome me!

I feel inside His Presence--
It's warm and friendly there!
His loving arms surround me--
He takes in all my care!

He loves me more, it seems,
Than I shall ever know--
As I look back upon the past,
At the blessings He has bestowed!

Jesus is my Good Friend!
He's always there for me!
The good thing is, if I need Him,
He's there - Eternally!

Lorna Sparks Gutierrez

Inspiration Verse
Hebrews 13:5 (KJV)
Jesus said: "........I will never leave you, nor forsake you."!

Look To Jesus

Tell The Man all of your sorrows and hate!
He takes the crooked and makes things straight.
He takes the confusion and makes it all plain.
He's got salve for the soul - you can only gain!

I've found His promises to be true!
Hold onto to Him....Don't let go!
Tell Him you need and want Him....He's there!
All He asks is your heart and soul!

He's loving and kind and will do you no wrong.
He'll come into your heart and create a new song!
He is the One who wants to please us.
My dear friend, call Him - His name is JESUS!

He talks the Talk and walks the Walk!
You can, too - just do as He'd do!
Follow His Steps and watch His Ways,
Then, you'll be successful for the rest of your days!

Lorna Sparks Gutierrez

Inspirational Verses
John 8:32 (KJV)
"And you shall know the truth, and the truth will make you free."
Matthew 4:19 (KJV)
And He (Jesus) said unto them, "Follow me, and I will make you fishers of men."
1 Peter 2:21 (KJV)
"For even hereunto were ye called: because Christ also suffered for us, leaving us an example,
that we should follow His Steps."

Love Changes Things

Mr. Impatience walked in one day!
Patience - alone - gave him place.
Patience knew at once that this was the soul-mate of Disgrace!
Disgrace then moved rapidly in, and Patience left the room!
All that was left was the Family of Turmoil--
And Trouble was born too soon!

LOVE then knocked on the door, and of course,
Impatience *quickly* replied!
Too soon of course, for just one look at **LOVE**,
Then, Impatience *quickly* died!

Disgrace could then no longer be Disgrace--
BECAUSE LOVE CHANGES ALL!
Patience was revived again,
Because **LOVE** came to call!

Lorna Sparks Gutierrez

Inspirational Verses
The whole chapter of 1st Corinthians 13 (KJV)
And
Galatians 5:14 (KJV) which states, "for all the law is fulfilled in ONE word, even in this,
'Thou shalt LOVE thy neighbor as thyself.'"
I do believe that ONE word is LOVE!

Of Life's Experiences

Your heart may be a little cracked right now;
But, it's not totally broken!
Of experience, it leaves us at least,
Somehow, wisdom - its expensive token!

Take heart, for each thing in life leaves some kind of mark;
But, don't let it inscribe some terrible
inset upon your sweet heart!
Take what life gives - use it - but don't be used or abused.
Just see what good can come of it;
Reshape it, and give it some excuse!

When life gives you a lemon, then make lemonade.
And, if life's sun gets too hot, the Lord will provide the shade.
One experience in life should not your life ruin!
It should not even pace it; you should
be the one to set the tune!

Color your world the color you want;
Paint your pictures bright!
That's the only way you can make
Those pictures turn out just right!

Lorna Sparks Gutierrez

Inspirational Verses
Romans 8:28 (KJV)
"And we know that all things work together for good to them that love God,
to them who are the called, according to His purpose."
Proverbs 3:5-6
(5)"Trust in the Lord with all thine heart; and lean not unto thine own understanding.
(6) In all thy ways acknowledge Him, and He shall direct thy paths."

Of Prayer

My soul was hungry--
God's Love fell down on me.
I could feel His Spirit feed mine,
Blending and growing as stars in ecstasy!

****

Full of wonder, my heart full of joy,
No longer hungry nor left alone,
My spirit in flight - as from prayer I arose,
Ready to go forth - and help other hungry souls!

Lorna Sparks Gutierrez

On Answered Prayer

Have you ever prayed hard for something
That you felt you really needed to receive?
And, that it took God so long to answer,
You wondered if your faith was weak to believe?

And still, you knew that God was God--
For THAT you were sure!
But still, you wondered why this burden
Yet had to be endured!

Keep praying, dear one, for The Bible says,
"The fervent prayer of a righteous man availeth much"*
Yes, miracles I've seen - and heard
Of answered prayer and joyous such!

It's so hard for us to understand
When prayers aren't answered the way it should seem!
'Tis said, "All prayers are answered....just not the way we ween".
Some answers are "no" - some answers may be "wait";
But no matter, still we pray;
And, hope the answer is clear and not late!

While praying, we rant, we cry, we fuss,
And wallow in self-pity!
We try to find a justice by quoting well-suited ditties!
Sometimes I'm sure a person's misery may be justified;
And, we rely on some theory, trusted or tried!

Maybe it isn't totally, the prayers....although prayer is VERY important!
Maybe should be also TRUSTING God,
If we let Him lead in our deportment!
But of one thing, I am sure - I'll keep walking with my Lord God;
For, I need His Friendship and Love as I walk this earthen sod!

Lorna Sparks Gutierrez

Inspirational Verse
James 5:16 (KJV)
"........The effectual, fervent prayer of a righteous man availeth much!"

Note: I prayed for my husband's salvation for 46 years, and lived to see him baptized by his own desire!
You can dance with great joy over the promises of God, who did promise me 46 years earlier that
He (The Lord) would save my husband! What a marvelous Redeemer!

82

Success Plan

Good intentions are simply that--
That…and nothing more!
Neither do they get the job done by themselves,
Nor settle any score!

Determination must be teamed
In thought and in deed
With action, if any plan is to be accomplished,
Or any act is to succeed!

God also helps those who help themselves*, it's sometimes true!
With determination, prayer, and God's help, you'll see it thru!
So thru hard times, do not despair;
As Worse it seems, is always somewhere!

Be thankful for now, but determined
For better tomorrows;
For action with excitement and hope,
Will wipe away today's sorrows!

So, try this plan to see how you'll reach
Your heart's goal.
It'll add self-esteem, joy, and riches
To your hungry, eager soul!

Lorna Sparks Gutierrez

Inspirational Verse
Luke 1:37 (KJV)
And the angel of the Lord said unto Mary,
"For with God nothing shall be impossible."

*Note: Although I have not found a scripture that says God helps those who help themselves,
I know if you pray and trust Him, the praying and trusting is helping yourself!
In 1 Corinthians 4:12(KJV), St. Paul stated that he and his disciples labored, working with their own hands.
And, in Ephesians 4:28(KJV), St. Paul stated that one should "labor, working with his hands the thing which is good,
that he may have to give to him that needeth."
This is saying to me that we should work, not just for our own good, but for the good of others.

Poetry

To Make

One Think

C. Poetry to Make One Think

A Note To Impatience

Patience is a virtue;
Patience is a strength;
One must find it within his own self;
He can find it in a wink!

For manliness is strong
To fight against innumerable foes--
Enemies, within our own selves,
Which cause destructive woes!

But Hearken!
A remedy--
One's searching out the misery--
Replacing it with visionry--
That great wisdom from above,
The remedy is LOVE!

NOTE: God IS love!

Lorna Sparks Gutierrez

Inspirational Verses
Proverbs 29:11 (KJV)
A fool utters all his mind but a wise man keeps it in till afterwards.
Luke 21:19 (KJV)
In your patience possess ye your souls.

A Beauty of a Woman

Wherein does a woman's beauty lie?
Is it in a dimple or a wink of her eye?
Is it in soft or perfumed hair?
Where is her beauty - where - oh, where?

Wherein does a woman's beauty seem?
Is it in reality or in a dream?
Is it in a fine figure or a graceful walk?
Could it be in flirtatious and interesting talk?

Possibly in brains where she's maybe respected?
Or maybe in money where no lack is suspected?
Can a man trust his life to these outward expressions?
Or will he look further toward inward directions?

Would he look into a woman's soul
To find a good friend there - or just 'cold'?
Deep inside her soul he should find
A place there to comfort and calm his mind;

A place where he can withdraw to rest
Amidst life's confusions and tests.
Will he find kindness and a listening voice?
Will patience and thoughtfulness be virtue's choice?

Will she have morals in which he can trust?
For in us ALL, Trust is a Must!

In all this beauty, a man will seek for a mate.
But will this question be too late?
SHE will ask and look and mind;
For what does HE have to offer that is So Fine??

Lorna Sparks Gutierrez

Biblical Verses of Inspiration---Proverbs 31:1-31

Admiration In A Man

Charm, that twists the heart and flatters,
Is sometimes so deceitful, charm really doesn't matter!
Although I've seen some men who could use a little charm,
The truth of the matter is - there is no need for alarm!

Look past the flattering manner, past any light-hearted banter.
Does this man keep a promise he's given?
Honest in his dealings with men and women?
Can you give him an honest reference?
Would you trust him to your daughter's preference?

Is kindness, compassion, or patience an appeal?
Is he brave for honest labor?
Are his goals in life real?
Would you be able to trust his help, were you in a pinch?
Or would he answer in sarcasms that would make one wince?

Can you relax in the presence of his soul, with no fear?
And can you feel when he's around, that God is also near?
Then for that man - a woman should pray,
That in her life, he'll be her friend - and stay!

And if you are a man
That would want a woman to stay,
Then enroll these virtues in your life
As soon as possible......TODAY!

Lorna Sparks Gutierrez

Inspirational Verse
I Samuel 16:7 (KJV)
"......for man looks at the outward appearance, but the Lord looks on the heart."

Caring For My Friends

That part of my heart that I can give,
That part of my heart I will.

A handshake, a smile, a helpful hand,
Advice, conversation and still.....and still,
That is a part of my heart,

Love in many ways--
To show my friends that I do care
To know them for all their days!

Lorna Sparks Gutierrez

Inspirational Verse
Proverbs 18:24 (KJV)
"A man that has friends must show himself friendly, and there is a Friend who sticks closer than a brother."

Chunky

I thought that I was chunky,
Till I saw her standing on the street.
I knew she was miserable,
Although she seemed to be so neat!

She had a lovely face and was very nice;
But, she looked as tho she'd eaten 3 times her share of rice.
I thought to myself, "I'm sure also she must need
About 3 times her share of love - love is also feed".

I took that thought home with me.
So I thought I'd have for lunch:
A bowl of soup and for dessert, low-calorie punch.

But instead, I thought that I should take:
A bowl of compassion and a slice of kindness, instead of cake,
A little snack of thoughtfulness - the bread of a good deed--
And If I kept this diet up, I'd be slender as a reed!

So the next time you start to diet,
And temptation takes a hand,
Just substitute that sugar and fat
For the virtues of honorable man!

In no time at all you'll be slender, yes, it's true!
But what is more, there'll be....more beauty *inside* of you!

Lorna Sparks Gutierrez

Inspirational Verses

Proverbs 23:1-3 (KJV)
When you sit to eat with a ruler, consider diligently what is before you. And put a knife to your throat, if you be a man given to appetite. Do not be desirous of his dainties: for they are a deceitful food.

Note: I really don't want to put a knife to my throat; I'd rather just push myself away from the table. But people do not realize that eating wrong all the time, is just as deadly as putting a knife to your throat! Eating wrongly hurts, and I should know (I am guilty - too)!

Exasperation - A Note

I can be stubborn…I'll admit it's true;
But, how many others have to put up with you?

You bicker and quarrel and find fault at every angle;
When it comes to help me, 'tis sure, out of it you'll wrangle.

I really - really wonder at times
What I should do.
If I gave you away, you'd just make another
Woman a shrew.

You're like a little child - you can't make up your mind;
And, I'll ever wonder at what happiness you'll find.

I can only hope that one day,
That peace, you will find.
Maybe then I can also rest,
And we will both find some peace of mind!

Lorna Sparks Gutierrez

Inspirational Verse
Isaiah 41:10 (KJV)
"Fear thou not, for I am with thee: be not dismayed: for I am thy God; I will strengthen thee:
Yea, I will help thee: yea, I will uphold thee with the right hand of my righteousness."

Halloween-Halloween!

Halloween, Halloween, with witches and goblins galore!
Its Druid spirit catches the cold winds,
As it blows on its eerie folklore!
Stories tell of how it began - only the Ancient know for sure;
But even the Harmless celebrate it,
Not realizing the impact it may endure!

Demonic witches celebrate it some - in true, devilish delight--
Celebrating on into a distant cold dark night!
Holy Spirit sees forever - our spirits do not see so far or true;
But, He sees that Halloween is not Holy, and "et tu?"

I do not celebrate it now, altho I have before.
No one even needs a thought of bad spirits at his door!
I shan't celebrate it, and I'll be skeptical of those who try.
I believe that this tradition is one that Christ spoke of 'er nigh!
So think about this, be careful if you are of the Lord:
Can you still celebrate Halloween…and be to God in One Accord?

How about just a Harvest Party to celebrate Fall's arrival so hardy?
So, let the children safely run and celebrate Fall's fun--
In the beautiful eve of October's golden sun!
And I ask you for as what you do,
Would it be as Jesus - yes, He would do?
Think about this, as I have thought:
Did Jesus celebrate anything like this? I think naught!

Lorna Sparks Gutierrez

P.S. Call me a spoil-sport - you won't be the first! Ha-ha! And, many of you will not agree with me. Think on it, though!

Inspirational Verses:

Mark 7:7-13 (KJV) Jesus said, "And in vain do they worship Me, teaching for doctrines the commandments of men. 8 For laying aside the commandment of God, you hold the tradition of men, such as (the washing of pitchers and cups), and MANY OTHER SUCH THINGS YOU DO" 9 He said to them, "All too well you reject the commandment of God, that you may keep your tradition. 10 For Moses said, "Honor your father and your mother and, he who curses father or mother, let him be put to death". 11 But you say if a man says to his father or mother, "Whatever profit you might have received from me is Corban" (that is, a gift to God), 12 then you no longer let him do anything for his father or his mother, 13 MAKING THE WORD OF GOD OF NO EFFECT THROUGH YOUR TRADITION WHICH YOU HAVE HANDED DOWN. AND MANY SUCH THINGS YOU DO."

Ephesians 6:10-20, (NKJV), The Whole Armor of God, St. Paul said:
10" Finally, my brethren, be strong in the Lord and in the power of His might. 11 Put on the whole armor of God that you may be able to stand against the wiles of the devil. 12 For we do not wrestle against flesh and blood, but against principalities, against powers, against the rulers of the darkness of this age, against spiritual hosts of wickedness in the heavenly places. 13 Therefore take up the whole armor of God that you may be able to withstand in the evil day, and having done all, to stand.
14 Stand therefore, having girded your waist with truth, having put on the breastplate of righteousness, 15 and having shod your feet with the preparation of the gospel of peace; 16 above all, taking the shield of faith with which you will be able to quench all the fiery darts of the wicked one. 17 And take the helmet of salvation, and the sword of the Spirit, which is the word of God; 18 praying always with all prayer and supplication in the Spirit, being watchful to this end with all perseverance and supplication for all the saints— 19 and for me, that utterance may be given to me, that I may open my mouth boldly to make known the mystery of the gospel, 20 for which I am an ambassador in chains; that in it I may speak boldly, as I ought to speak."
Also read Matthew 15:1-9

Note: All this is a Harvest of Spiritual Thought!

Hospitality in a Hospital

I came to her room to draw her blood.
Her nurse said she couldn't comprehend or feel.
However, I treated her as tho she could.
I'm glad, for what I tell is real!
I said, "Mrs. Jones, I need to draw your blood;
And, I'll be as careful as I can be."--
Then I proceeded to do my job
Very tenderly!

Afterwards, when I was through,
I whispered in her ear,
"Maybe you can't hear, but your spirit can,
And I will pray for you, my dear."
I prayed for God to bless
This person hurt and worn,
That God would heal and comfort,
That she could feel His love so warm!

When I was through, I smiled.
And although she could not move,
A tear proceeded to drop by drop
Down her cheek as I left the room.
I turned to wipe her tear with a tissue,
And told her I'd keep her in my prayers.
Then I wondered at the issue,
That her soul had senses there!

No matter if a person
Is broken, torn or hurt,
Whether mentally or physically,
We've no right to be cold or a jerk!
Further we should take it
To treat others as good as we'd like.
But more, as we'd like to be treated--
So shun cold wrong - It's better to do right!

So think this thought, dear caretaker--
Some day you may be in that place!
And you will want your keeper
To care for you with dignity and grace!

Lorna Sparks Gutierrez

Inspirational Verse: Matthew 7:12 (KJV)
Jesus said,
"Therefore all things whatsoever ye would that men should do to you, do ye even so to them:
for this is the law and the prophets."

How Not To Raise A Gang Member

Teach a child to look up!
God and Heaven are there;
Then he'll get the idea
Someone up there cares!

Teach a child to pray;
Then, he'll know whom to ask.
Remind him everyday
That prayer's a privilege, not a task!

Teach a child to love.
Teach a child to care.
Show him Love yourself.
Teach him how to share.

Teach a child right from wrong,
And teach him manly ways.
Teach him Strength's singular song*
That powers his life's ways!

But more than all - Teach him God!--
The Source of manly power!
The child will grow into a man, as a rod.
He'll stand for Right - honoring Life's hour!

Lorna Sparks Gutierrez

Inspirational Verses
Proverbs 22:6 (KJV)
"Train up a child in the way he SHOULD go: and when he is old, he will not depart from it."!
Nehemiah 8:10 (KJV), "....For the Joy of the Lord is your Strength."
*For me, Strength's Singular song is joy in the Lord.

It All Comes Down to Love

(written for those who care and take care of others)

To be one who bears for another's life,
There shall be stress - there shall be strife!

The lessons learned shall not be long,
The lessons are there to make us strong!

The Good we do will help another,
Even-tho at times we may think it a bother!

But the Lord said we must not forget the Love--
Or the work will be for us as nothing--
(No blessing from *ABOVE*).

A sacrifice of *LOVE* it all must bring,
To lessen Life's frequent and horrid stings!

But just remember, *LOVE* grows our spirits.
LOVE adds happiness *ALSO* to *SELF*,
And to *SELF*, the *LOVE* will cheer it!

Lorna Sparks Gutierrez

Inspirational Verse
1 Corinthians 13:3
(NIV)
"If I give all I possess to the poor and give over my body to hardship that I may boast,
and do not have LOVE, I gain NOTHING!"

Jesus, Sweet Lover Of My Soul

Your Love to me fulfills my longing.
Empty places in my heart You fill.

You care for me as no other only.
Your love for me truly can and will.

My future is Yours and my love solely,
Belong to Thee for Thy use only.

No other will do, as I belong to You.
Oh Jesus...sweet lover of my soul!

Sweet Friend, Sweet Brother!
Sweet Father, Sweet Lover!
Oh Jesus, Sweet Lover of my soul!

Lorna Sparks Gutierrez

Inspirational Verse
John 15:9 (KJV)
Jesus said:
"As the Father hath loved Me, so have I loved you: continue ye in My love."

Jesus Waltzed Me Across Heaven!

I had the most beautiful dream last night!
Religious critics would have swooned from the sight!
Only This ONE could know how I loved to dance!
How happy He made me as we swirled and pranced.

For This ONE had taken me in His arms,
And waltzed me across the Floor with miraculous charms!
I was in a Golden Place.
You could feel the Love as we embraced.

Such Love so unaffected, so pure I felt in my heart.
So Good and Clean, as should be whole, not as in part!
This ONE was swirling me across Heaven's golden floor.
I had entered a place of Pure Love - thru Heaven's door!

Suddenly I fell at the Master's feet,
And was worshipping Jesus, my God, So Sweet!
Before I hadn't realized exactly who He was--
Yet in my heart I knew, This ONE was from Above!

There is nothing like a sweet dream of Peace--
And nothing like dreaming of Jesus, His Spirit's Sweet Release.*
I hope I'll dream of Him again tonight--
Another adventure with Jesus, the God of Love and Light!

Maybe tonight we'll picnic by Heaven's crystal waterfall.
Perhaps I'll visit with other Saints, and
Memories of Christ's Goodness we'll recall.

Perchance the Lord will have a party--
And He'll invite me too!
We'll celebrate all over Heaven--
'Twould be the Saintly thing to do!

But should I dream of Jesus,
I know all will be alright!--
As I dream of beautiful adventures
With Jesus my Lord, tonight!

Lorna Sparks Gutierrez

Inspirational Verses
Ecclesiastes 3:1, 4 (KJV)
Verse 1: "To everything there is a season, and a time to every purpose under the heaven."
Verse 4: ".., and a time to DANCE."
Psalms 149:3 (KJV)
Let them praise His name in the dance; Let them sing praises unto Him with the timbrel and harp.
*The Sweet Release of the Lord is His Giving to us of the Holy Spirit, which one can truly feel!

Just for Today

Just for today
I will do my best!--
And things I cannot help,
God will have to do the rest.

When times get rough,
And there seems no rest--
When I'm not up to par,
And I feel I may fail of a test--

Tomorrow is hope
In that, I may re-invest;
And get the strength to try
To enjoy a bit of life's zest!

--And rest and rest--
And wait for the best!

Lorna Sparks Gutierrez

Inspirational Verse
Isaiah 40:31 (KJV)
"But they that WAIT upon the Lord shall renew their strength; they shall mount up with wings as eagles;
they shall run, and not be weary; they shall walk, and not faint."

Las Cosas Preciosas
(The Precious Things)

Things too familiar to us often become commonplace;
These familiar "cosas" may be taken for granted,
Their value not appreciated at its face.

What values are these?
We need really to think in our little minds!
So what would it take us to think?
What would be the signs?

Do we need to feel the pain of loss?
Or else we may not count the precious costs?

Heaven forbid!
Look with new eyes to the "cosas" that are ours:
Our family, friends, our lives, even the hours!

Even time, memories cherished and not so bright--
Let's with appreciation make our memories somehow aright!

Appreciation now, with new eyesight, cleansed and reborn--
Our "cosas" not taken for granted,
With an attitude spiritually reformed!

Lorna Sparks Gutierrez

Inspirational Verse
Colossians 3:15 (KJV)
Saint Paul said, "And let the peace of God rule in your hearts,..................and be ye thankful."!

Peaceful Free Existence

My desire upon them that hate me,
Is to see them love the Lord!--
To see them as my brother
As we walk in one accord.
The Lord is on my side;
But, I must be on His side too.--
For, 'tis better to walk together in love,
Than to be contentious and therefore, fools!
It's better to go to Life's school
To learn about the Almighty Lord,
Than to die in sin's misery
Or perish with evil's own sword!
Pray Lord, give us wisdom
To live this Life much better--
To be free of sin's heavy shackles--
To rid our back of Burden's fetters!
There is comfort to be had,
There is Lightness for you and me,
For Jesus Christ the Savior
Came to set us sinners free!

Lorna Sparks Gutierrez

Pebbles Of Life's Strife

Walking along "The Beach of Life",
I stumbled upon some pebbles of strife.
I knew they were mine,
But what good were they for?
I'd throw them in the water,
But they'd just float back upon the shore!

I could collect them and build myself a fire--
Or roast wieners upon it, and be warmed by its bier!
I would not let them stay under my feet;
I'd put them in order and keep it all neat!
So brother, if troubles collect and get all under afoot,
Remember the fire, and don't get so shook!

Don't let strife get you under control.
Don't let it anger you deep within your soul.
Have a good talk with God--
He'll show you how!
Don't wait, stressed out person!
Do it right now!

Lorna Sparks Gutierrez

Inspirational Verse
Psalm 17:6 (KJV)
"I have called upon thee, for thou wilt hear me, O God! Incline thine ear unto me, and hear my speech."

People By The Wayside

There are people who fall by the wayside.
They seem helpless; it seems so.
Do we help them to a better Somewhere?
Have we done our best? I don't know!

With foul tongue and slander,
People push others further down.
It seems some are never happy,
Until someone crumbles to the ground!

But the person wise and willful--
And with conscience to his God--
Will pick them up so wisely--
And replant them on solid sod!

A plant with a little sun and water,
A little care and love,
Will thrive to grow and not falter,
As a person who…*receives love.*

Care as you can, if some will let you;
For some will, and some will NOT!--
For in the end, we ALL have to answer
To God, for what we've wrought!

Lorna Sparks Gutierrez

Inspirational Verse
Matthew 5:7 (KJV)
"Blessed are the merciful; for they shall obtain mercy."

Perfect Imperfection

I'm not perfect,
No matter how much I'd like so to think!
Just when I think I am,
I fall faster than an eye can blink!

I just might rub someone
Just the wrong way!
Or frown unknowingly, offendingly,
To someone one day.

Or I might say something
Someone doesn't like,
Or disagree with a matter a mite!

I might miss something
I should have done,
Or have done something differently
Than they'd have done.

Nevertheless, even though my heart
Is usually in the right place,
It's possible I can be wrong,
Not even near Life's Ace!

I can be off target, but I can trust God,
To put me back on;
If I just humble myself in prayer
To hear His Voice alone.

But I have this hope
And I will not regret,
That I can do better next time,
For Life is not over yet!

Lorna Sparks Gutierrez

Inspirational Verse
Romans 3:23-24 (KJV)
23 For all have sinned, and come short of the Glory of God.
24 Being justified freely by His grace through the redemption that is in Christ Jesus.

Politics

When elections are up for grabs,
Politicians turn on each other
With pundits and back-stabs.

Of course, life is not perfect,
And neither are people;
But they are all put together
As a church with a steeple!

There are the good and the bad
All shuffling along,
Each attempting to take control
As to what is right or is wrong!

People disagree as to which is what,
To choose the superior
In deed or in thought!

They're resorting to fighting like immature children,
Disgusting their audience that's thinking there's no hope for them!
Possibly they have more money than common sense.
We all hope for someone who appears as less dense!

As people are people we will try to choose
The best - and leave the rest to God for Him to test;
So with good success and lots of prayer,
We must elect someone with less error.

Then, hope that this politician will get some
Good done - before it is too late--
As survival of our future generations is at stake!

Lorna Sparks Gutierrez

Inspirational Verses
1st. Peter 2:13-15 (KJV)
(13) "Submit yourselves to every ordinance of man for the Lord's sake: whether it be to the king as supreme;
(14) or unto governors, as unto them that are sent by him for the punishment of evil doers, and for the praise
*   of them that do well.*
(15) For so is the will of God, that with well doing ye may put to silence, the ignorance of foolish men."
Also read all of Romans chapter 13!

Right Thing - Right Time

The crispy breeze caressed my face,
As I tasted the water so cool.
I expressed to God thankfulness
For this blessing - better than a precious jewel.

For when you need a drink of cool water,
And a cool breeze upon your face,
A precious jewel just won't get it!
There's time for each thing - in each its own place!

Lorna Sparks Gutierrez

Inspirational Verse

Ecclesiastes 3:1 (KJV),

"To everything there is a season, and a time to every purpose under the heaven:"
Note:
Have a heart and read the whole chapter; I do believe you will enjoy it!

Side By Side With Jesus

I was somewhat cowardly and didn't want anyone to know, it's true--
That I was afraid of "this one and that thing", but Jesus, my Lord, He knew!
He blessed me one night and showed me myself in a dream.
The revelations were astonishing - they hit the spot, it seemed.

In the dream I was running from the devil and his villainous crew.
I was running harry-scary, so fast, I didn't know exactly what to do!
I ran up and down stairs - through alleys and streets,
Trying to find a hiding place where all would be safe and discreet!

The devil was big, and his cohorts were too!
Those who followed him did just as that old scoundrel would do!--
And then up a ways my eyes spotted the Lord!
Christ was chatting with His own companion, big as He!--
And they were in one accord.

I knew at once where safety dwelt!
I'd be small enough to fit under His garment's hem, I felt.
He didn't quit His conversation until He was done.
He didn't miss a Step or slow His Pace - the Peace would be won!

Jesus kept ahead of the devil - he didn't weary the Lord!
My Lord has the strength - no slackness He would afford!
After His talk, Jesus looked down at me and smiled.
I knew He probably thought I was a weak Christian child.

By the power of His Spirit, He spoke to me without uttering a word.
Now let me tell you these beautiful, glorious, spiritual words I heard!
"My child, I know you are so weak and small;
But, you can be like My friend here beside Me, and be strong and spiritually tall."

"Just do as he does, walk with Me and follow My Steps;
My Holy Spirit will give you the strength you need,
And also give you My Rest."
Then I awoke, no longer afraid - For Jesus dwells with me!
I no longer have to be a coward - For I walk with Christ, you see!

Lorna Sparks Gutierrez

Inspirational Verse
1 Peter 2:21 (NKJV)
For to this were you called, because Christ also suffered for us, leaving us an example, that you should follow His Steps.

Someone's Mother

Someone's mother was wise I know.
She witnessed in the lives of the children she sowed.
Her work was a pleasure - not a dreadful chore.
The influence reached to even the children next door.

Another's person's life would not have been better,
Had she neglected to write him a kind, thoughtful letter.
She'd even take time to meet another's need;
Often filling the hunger of a family she'd feed.

Her heart was generous - her humor was kind.
I imagine her patience was tested time after time.
An occasion or two I saw her lose it;
And I thought to myself, "she's human", in amusement!

I saw her tears, an occasional time, or two--
And I saw her in repentance as her heart she tried to renew.
If I had a problem she'd talk and pray with me.
She'd correct and encourage - with me, play occasionally.

I was fortunate to have known her.
She'd condescend to see my way.
She was my next door neighbor.
Her influence stays with me today.

Lorna Sparks Gutierrez

Note
Although I never saw my neighbor "lose it" (as I did so many times), she "fit the bill" as a Godly example of a Christian woman. Her name was Pearl Guinn. I am sure God told her, "Well done, my good and faithful servant!"
(mother of Donnie Guinn Cordrey and Sue Guinn Merritt, very sweet people also!)
And, thank you Pearl, for being my mother's good friend!

Temper – Temper

You allow that temper to fly--
It is inspired by satan--
He wants you to die!

It's obvious I see and,
You do not--
The devil wants to engulf you
In his schemish plot!

You must be *CAREFUL!*
You must deny him your place.
Else then your spirit
Will go in disgrace....!

Life is too short to give him an inch.
Just resist that old goat and make him flinch!
He'll flee from you--
(So, that's the wise thing to do)--

Then *YOU* will be Master of your Fate--
So control yourself *BEFORE* it's too late!

Lorna Sparks Gutierrez

Inspirational Verses

Proverbs 16:32 (KJV)
He that is slow to anger is better than the mighty; and he that rules his spirit is better than he that takes a city.

Also read Ephesians 4:26-27 (KJV)
(26)"Be ye angry, and sin not: let not the sun go down upon your wrath: (27) neither give place to the devil."

Note: The Lord is our Shield and our Defender; so, choose to walk with and to follow God.

Thanksgiving's Bounty

I love Thanksgiving - so much to celebrate!
Beautiful Autumn - the air is so crisp!
Darkness falling on us Early instead of Late--
Grey days seem greyer with haziness thru the mist!

Amber leaves, laced with gold and red,
Bunching up on lawns in piles--
Thru them my feet could gaily tread,
To walk happily mile upon mile!

I breathe deeply of cooler air.
The blood runs excitedly thru my veins--
While Harvest pumpkins, squash, and apples share
The girth of sunny golden grains!

Paper turkeys hang in decoration on school walls.
Excited children dream of big enormous feasts.
I see ahead labor and all it entailing-ly enthralls,
The planning, cooking, cleaning, and as for rest - the least!

We gather together with family and friends to gab.
Swap stories to enjoy and our fun enliven.
That solemn moment will be taken for God,
Our Thanksgiving for blessings He's given!

Each moment I'll enjoy - not by myself,
For God is with me every minute to share!
His Joy is the greatest blessing of wealth!--
For, I'm blessed with the Lord's Presence everywhere!

Lorna Sparks Gutierrez

Inspirational Verse
Psalms 13:6 (KJV)
(King David said),
"I will sing unto the Lord, because He hath dealt bountifully with me."

That Great Love

Kept me going when times got rough.
It gave me strength, and helped me to be tough.
That Great Love caused me to care.
It made me work to earn, and my goods to share.
That Great Love made me share all of my heart.
It pushed me to strive - to do my part.
That Great Love fed me when my soul was lean.
It kept me from falling and being so mean.
It caused me to be honest, even when it hurt--
With myself or others, oneself to assert.
That Great Love came from Jesus, the Father of Lights,
The Giver of Hope, the Giver of Life,
Who hung on the Cross for our weaknesses and sin;
Who gave Love no other man could, Love without end!
Love that flowed from Calvary's Cross to lonely Man,
To fill men with Hope, that needs demand!
I'm so thankful for that Love every day--
All I have to do is simply PRAY!--
Great Love is what Christ gave for you and me.
NOW we have hope of Heaven and Eternity!

Lorna Sparks Gutierrez

Inspirational Verse
Psalms 106:1 (KJV)
Praise ye the Lord, Oh give thanks unto the Lord; for He is good; for His mercy endureth forever.

The Captain Of My Soul

More than all the world to me,
To Him I give my destiny.

I salute Him - Yes!
And love Him more.

My all I give;
Him I adore!

He is my God; and my soul, He keeps.
In Him I live in shallows and in deeps.

This earth may roam and take its toll--
Still, Christ is the Captain of my soul!

Lorna Sparks Gutierrez

The Depths Of Hell

One night I dreamed that my soul fell.
It fell in a void, desolate as Hell.
No one was there - it was dark - it was deep.
My soul was suspended - the abyss was steep.

I saw no bottom, but I was sure that I was there!
Where was someone to help me - where was someone to care?
I cried out to God; surely, He could hear my cry!--
Then I awoke in bed - so glad I had not died!

Surely the dream was for something?
But I could not it explain!
Had someone else just been there, to visit satan's claim?
Suddenly I felt for them - I knew 'twas not for me.
Someone needed to be prayed for, so I got down on my knees.

I asked God to watch over, whoever it might be!
I didn't know who it was, but God - He could see!
"Please God", I cried for them, "Oh save their soul from Hell!
Send angels to guide and guard them, to keep them safe and well."

When the anguish left me, I knew I had prayed alright.
Calm overtook me, and I rested better that night.
My spirit told me that maybe someone had taken dope.
That he had been in the presence of satan's fearsome coke.

So I left that prayer with God - but continued to pray in my heart--
That satan would leave that one alone, that he'd be delivered from the dark!
God had wanted me to know of the danger that the child was in--
That it was edged ever so deeply - so much worse than some other sins!

And then a neighbor told me that her son was gone.
She was worried and afraid, everything seemed so wrong!
So we prayed and fasted together--THAT broke old satan's attack!
Then she received a phone call, asking if she wanted her son back!

So, if you feel the urge to pray for someone, then don't hesitate!
The Lord will surely hear you - the answer won't be late!
And don't, dear friend, dabble in dope - satan's fearsome guise!
Remember my stint in the depths of Hell - remember, and be wise!

Lorna Sparks Gutierrez

(True story)

Inspirational Verses
Psalms 139: 8,12 (KJV)
8. If I ascend up into heaven, Thou art there: if I make my bed in hell, behold, Thou art there.
12. Yea, the darkness hideth not from Thee; but the night shineth as the day: the darkness and the light are both alike to Thee.

The Desert Wind

The Desert Wind has its own genre to blend,
As it blows hither and there.
And altho I feel displaced,
Memories don't erase; they beckon everywhere.

But the desert can be warm,
Or hot or cold,
Depending on where your heart is!
Love will abound,
And our hearts will turn around,
To be where God wants us to live.

I love the wind.
The sun's warmth will lend.
But, I deem both can be so cruel!
Just as we, eyeing Eternity,
Allow whatever's in our hearts to rule!

The wise man will harness it all:
The sun, the wind, the rain!
Just as we must do--our souls--to conquer too!
For our eternity, we mustn't profane!

I feel God everywhere in the desert, dry air.
He hasn't forsaken His own!
There is still work to do,
If we love Him too;
For, there is a harvest left yet to atone!

God is in the wind.
I feel His Presence as He blends
In those I feel and see!
My spirit soars long but not alone!
For, the Desert Wind blows its song to me!

Lorna Sparks Gutierrez

Inspirational Verse
2nd Samuel 22:11 (NKJV)
He rode upon a cherub, and flew; and He (God) was seen upon the wings of the wind!

The Grouch!

The grouch, the grouch, the spiritual slouch!
Unhappy with self, hateful with others!
Scrooge of the soul - Oh, Misery's lover!

Squinter of the eye, hateful of soul!
Acid of tongue, too loose, too bold!
The grouch, the grouch, the miserable slouch!

But God has a Finger to change with a touch!
Love overcomes, the chemistry's done!
Oh where, Oh where is the slouch,
Misery's grouch?

In humbleness he left, vanished from sight!
'Twas changed in an instant,
As he saw Christ, the Light!

No more Misery's lover,
But Peace's fate!
He's grinning, laughing, loving--
He's Beauty's own mate!

The grouch? He's changed - excited - reformed!
He's no longer the same - he's been Reborn!

Lorna Sparks Gutierrez

Inspirational Verses
John 3: 7-8 (KJV)
(Jesus said) "Marvel not that I say unto thee, Ye must be born again. The wind bloweth where it listeth, and thou hearest the sound thereof. But canst not tell whence it cometh, and whither it goeth: so is every one that is born of the Spirit."

2 Corinthians 5:17 (KJV)
Therefore if any man be in Christ, he is a new creature: old things are passed away; behold, all things are become new.

(This poem was written for my husband, whom the Lord promised to me that He would save him!) And He did!

The Horoscope

I do believe that some psychics can tell you many things;
But trusting them instead of God--
To which do you cling?
I realize that psychics do possess a gift.
I also realize that many gifts exist.
But, if you do not use them to serve the Creator of the Universe,
Anything less than serving God, could be considered worse!

I had to learn a lesson in a very hard way.
To trust God or not - there was a price to pay!
The cost was the loss of a relationship with Jesus my Lord.
The cost of THAT loss I could not afford!

I know that it is tempting to read the Daily Horoscope.
Many look to it in weak faith to find some hope.
But, the Holy Spirit truly gives us wisdom to receive.
The Horoscope is not of Christ - it's satan's way to deceive.
Our God is a jealous God - Christ says to look to Him.
He told us not to look to seers - that trust is slim.
When we receive Christ's Spirit, He speaks to His own.
He freely gives us wisdom - that wisdom is renown.

I know the horoscopes are tempting, but we must obey.
If we are truly to be Christ's, we must hear Him today--
So, DAILY read that BIBLE, and spend daily time in PRAYER--
And listen to the Holy Spirit - do you DARE?
So get down and get with it - OBEY the Christ.
Don't let the devil take you on a tangent heist!
Some people have psychic gifts that are given by God;
But, make sure it's Jesus they serve - only ONE Spirit - That of God!

So, I pray for psychics and mediums, and for others do I pray--
For God to save them, as well as me, do I say.
I cannot them the gifts to judge, except for what the Bible says.
For, I once thought I possessed some psychic gift--
When It was just the Holy Spirit in me to assist.
So, if you need a Scope to look to - Look to Christ.
He has the Graphic Guide to Eternal Life.
His Daily Word of the Bible will guide your way.
And so in learned wisdom, I quietly have nothing more to say!
Except to PRAY and OBEY.

Lorna Sparks Gutierrez

<u>Note:</u>
Renown people in the Old Bible who seemed to possess seer-like and prophetic powers were: Elisha, Elijah, Isaiah, Jeremiah, Samuel, Daniel, and at one point King Saul prophesied, even King David. There were others, also. In the New Testament were such people as the Lord, his 12 disciples, and Paul of Tarsus. However, the point is, they served GOD! There were other prophets also, listed as major and minor prophets.

The Horoscope Inspirational Verses

Inspirational Verses
Deuteronomy 18:9-14
King James Version (KJV) Old Testament (Old Covenant)
9 When thou art come into the land which the Lord thy God giveth thee, thou shalt not learn to do after the abominations of those nations.
10 There shall not be found among you any one that maketh his son or his daughter to pass through the fire, or that useth divination, or an observer of times, or an enchanter, or a witch.
11 Or a charmer, or a consulter with familiar spirits, or a wizard, or a necromancer.
12 For all that do these things are an abomination unto the Lord: and because of these abominations the Lord thy God doth drive them out from before thee.
13 Thou shalt be perfect with the Lord thy God.
14 For these nations, which thou shalt possess, hearkened unto observers of times, and unto diviners: but as for thee, the Lord thy God hath not suffered thee so to do.
Proverbs 16:33 (TLB), The Living Bible
We toss the coin, but it is the Lord who controls its decision.
(NKJV), The lot is cast into the lap, But its every decision is from the Lord.

For those seeking One who can save you if you are wandering around lost: read the verses below:
New Testament (New Covenant) (KJV)
Matthew 18:11, For the Son of man (Jesus) is come to save that which was lost.
Luke 19:10, For the Son of man is come to seek and to save that which was lost.

Concerning the Gifts of the Holy Spirit:
Galatians 3:28 (NKJV) St. Paul said, "For the gifts and calling of God are irrevocable."
Galatians 3:28 (AKJV) St. Paul said, "For the gifts and calling of God are without repentance."

Note the difference between the Old Covenant and the New Covenant.
Although God doesn't change, He made a New Covenant through the Advent and Crucifixion of His Son, Jesus Christ, Who was considered God Incarnate, the Living Word. Now by accepting Jesus Christ as our Savior, we are saved from our sins and saved from eternal death!

Think Who Gives

Most times we're so busied
With thoughts of our concerns,
That we forget to give thanks
For little blessings and trials in which one learns.

We take time for our own rest and pleasure,
And take thought for future leisure;
But, where is God in all of this thought?
Does He cross our minds, seldom or oft?

Daily, we should give thanks
For where we are in society's ranks.
For without God, we'd be nowhere,
Without His love - without His constant care!

Gratefulness is not that hard--
Ever do without, and you'll see
That you'll think, and not take for granted,
God's gifts He gives to you and me!

Lorna Sparks Gutierrez

Inspirational Verse
1 Corinthians 2:9 (KJV)
(St. Paul said)" But as it is written,' Eye hath not seen, nor ear heard, neither have entered into the heart of man, the things which God hath prepared for them that love Him'."

118

Thou Shalt Not Bully!

Some people seem to think that when the Lord said,
"Do unto others as you would have them do unto you",
That somehow that did not apply to them! They misunderstood.
They didn't seem to see the relationship, not as they should!
Bullying isn't just at school - bullying breaks the Golden Rule.
To do unto others as you should, to rise to greater heights,
Then indeed you would!

To break another's heart - you should not be glad.
To lower yourself at a lesser level - that should make you sad!
Hurt done to others sometimes cannot be undone,
Pain so deep from being so shunned!
Children need to learn before the age of three,
While sitting at the feet of their parents' knees,
That to be wise and to be good,
Makes us happy and freer, as it should!

SO BE FIRMLY ALERTED!
When quickly attention is given to such a situation,
Much sadness could be averted.
Some people do not realize that to be mean and cruel
Is killing another's soul; that - you and I should rue!
And some really do die from cruel remarks
That others have aimed at their tender hearts!

Knowledge makes us wise - don't snub it - do not it despise.
Don't turn away your head; don't turn away your heart.
Meet bullying headlong; its arrogance should be de-thronged!*
Arrogance is the set-up for any bullying stage.
Arrogance gives birth to any son of rage.
Rage doesn't think well; it doesn't put itself in your place.
Rage has to be halted - before a life is displaced!

There is only one remedy for bullying's display:
Replace bullying with KINDNESS - each and every day!
Remember Bullying doesn't just walk at school.
ANYWHERE you see him, Bullying breaks the Golden Rule!
Also, if you stand by and see Bullying thrive,
You put yourself at risk, and even others' lives.
You must stand up for the person under duress.
Don't be guilty; you must pass Life's Tests!

A bully is an ignorant coward, who will someday attest,
That had he had more sense, he would not have been under arrest!
And he will surely pay for his sins, in remembrance, it never ends....
Perhaps if he could go back and redo it all again,
He would then not have to make amends.
Pray for God to help you to be smart;
Then, you will not have to live with guilty sorrow on your heart!
And thank the Lord that He, the Lord - is willing to forgive.
The Lord will forgive a bully if he's repentant of his sins!

Lorna Sparks Gutierrez

Inspirational Verses

Galatians 6:7 (NKJV)
"Be not deceived, God is not mocked; for whatever a man sows, that he will also reap."
Matthew 7:12 (NKJV)
Therefore whatever you want men to do to you, do also to them: for this is the Law and the Prophets.
*De-thronged, a poetic word for 'undoing the mob action', or 'dismantling the throng' (mob).

To Be Or Not To Be.....Up To Us?

We have to learn to be flexible,
To bend and not to break--
To be stronger, tenable,
And thereby, alter fate!

I heard if life gives you a lemon,
Then make lemonade.
A slice of lemon by itself adds spice;
Sometimes, just a touch adds strength to life.

If we've never had any adversity,
We'd be smug, spoiled, and unrefined.
Some of us must attend "Life's University,"
To mature, to grow, to be defined!

Life is how you look at it.
It's not just the questions that are asked;
But, how we answer them that's fit.
That will show how far we'll last!

However, 'tis a relief
When fate blows better winds!
You'll see a smile upon one's face,
When better things God sends!

Problems can be problems,
Or they can be stepping stones.
It all depends on how one walks--
To stay - or to go on......!

Lorna Sparks Gutierrez

To Conquer Anger

My anger sometimes controls me,
But never does it console me!
It, I must take by rein
To conquer, or else ne'er complain,

Of silly thought: that weakness would win the battle long!
But, with The Almighty's help, I can be strong
To win o'er the foe of any mind--
And my prize - "Virtue's Victory" sublime!

And Peace - the side effect to claim--
This prize to win o'er Anger's blame!

Lorna Sparks Gutierrez

To Differ

Each one has an offer to give,
A plan in life to enrich the other.
Why can't we then work together?
Why do we do mean things to our brother?

Is selfish sin the center of our hearts?
Before Christ - ourselves - we choose to see.
So in selfish misery, we seem to dwell
To suffer in sin - our own place to be!

It can be changed if we humble ourselves.
And in Christ's heart, *His* place we choose to dwell.
We can see loving Heaven on Earth to live,
And avoid the destination and miseries of Hell.

Peace is ours - ours only if we choose.
To do less - is verily to lose.
We must fight ourselves for peace, also rather--
And humble ourselves to love our brothers.

Take a hand out to God - hold Him close.
Your eyes will change - as will your heart also.
Walk in the Lord's Steps each day--
Then, Love will guide your thoughts - and your way!

Lorna Sparks Gutierrez

To Lighten The Load

Sometimes you have to have
Faith that God will see "it" thru.
Just let some things go their own way;
But, you go yours - the way that's true.

Let them be, for you cannot all change.
Maybe convince, maybe influence, maybe rearrange--
What? Get your own total way? Get real!
Sometimes we have to bend - not break - so just chill!

Let a few winds blow over your back--
And go with the flow of daily attacks.
That blood pressure may just get less;
And those nerves may relax, and you'll be less depressed!

Take a long look at it all; consider it to be deftly dealt.
Take it wisely, thoughtfully; and, be cool with yourself.
It may turn out better than you thought.
You'll see - things should get better than naught!

Lorna Sparks Gutierrez

Inspirational Verses:
Proverbs 3:5-6 (NKJV)
Trust in the Lord with all your heart, and lean not unto your own understanding; in all your ways acknowledge Him, and He shall direct your paths.

To See As God Sees

Lord, help me to love others as You love me.
And help me to see them as You see.
For, my mind cannot see into another's soul--
My eyes can only see as far as they go.

If someone doesn't just strike me just right,
Or something about them irritates me a mite--
Then, help me to use good judgment with caution;
And, let me be kind with actions, as unctuous.

Let me pray in believing faith for others.
Give me wisdom to deal with needs of another.
Judgment, wisdom, sensibility, and love:
These are good gifts from God above!

Lorna Sparks Gutierrez

Unequally Yoked

My heart is weary - somehow it seems
My heartache never ends.
I've prayed, threatened, and even declared,
But the answer No One sends!

"I love you, I love you." - my heart cries and bleeds.
But our lives are far apart, not sufficing our needs!

The thing that gives you life - it destroys mine.
What gives me peace is boredom to you.
I pray for God to show me a sign,
And to tell me exactly what I should do.

'Tis said that one must live and let live;
And when two are one, it should be easy to give.
Now when one knows how he has hurt his lover,
Their two hearts are cut to the core of each other.

I speak my heart - either way I lose.
If I let you go - how do I choose?
And, if I let you be – part of me dies?
You say you won't change - you verily vie!

You think I'm crazy - and I wonder about you!--
It's simply because of different points of view.
I ask myself if you are sick - or just me.
Only God knows the answer - Will He intervene?

I wish The Holy Spirit would speak to your heart.
I've loved you from the beginning - I never wanted us to part.
I realize lives are sometimes sad - it's true.
I can only pray God will show us what to do.

When two are pulled in differing thoughts - not so same:
Their lives are apart - their endeavors - inane.
The same goals, the same dreams are not truly theirs,
Creating sadness, these lives - not really shared.

Will this misery ever end? I can only hope!
Where, where is the answer to this sad anecdote?

Lorna Sparks Gutierrez

Inspirational Verse
2 Corinthians 6:14 (NKJV)
Do not be unequally yoked together with unbelievers.
For what fellowship has righteousness with lawlessness?
And what communion has light with darkness?

Weighty Matters At Thanksgiving

Everyone (it seems) is obsessed with his or her own weight!
People want to be thin before it's too late.
With Thanksgiving coming, it's going to be hard
Not to add pounds that turn into pure lard!

Pumpkin pie and all so spi-cet-ies--
Tempting dishes with all the ni-cet-ies!
If it's too cool to walk, I'd rather sit and dream
Of chocolate desserts covered with crèmes!

Maybe I should dream of a better figure so nice!
"On second thought, Sis, forget that other slice!"
Instead of dessert (forbid the thought!),
Let's go (past the bakery, of course) for a nice little walk--

Down to where the lonely are:
The hungry, the impaired, and the maimed.
The food that's left, the love that's left,
Forever our hearts should share the same.

The heart of a soul could use a pound or two.
I'd rather give some pie to him.
It's better to give of ourselves,
Than to live in selfish misery and sin!

I can be happy this Thanksgiving, and so can you!
If we just listen to our hearts,
That little conscience there should direct us what to do!

Lorna Sparks Gutierrez

Inspirational Verse
1 Corinthians 6: 19-20 (KJV)
19. What? Know ye not that your body is the temple of the Holy Ghost which is in you, which ye have of God, and ye are not your own? 20. for ye are bought with a price: therefore glorify God in your body, and in your spirit, which are God's.

Why Be Unhappy?

In misery we awake.
We spread it before our own.
We withdraw our hand from God--
When we should dial Him
Upon Heaven's phone!

God would give us a word
To guide this day.
The Truth is already there you know--
In the Bible, our Directory to Happiness,
To light our way!

The Word will put joy in your heart--
As joy wells up – ne'er to depart--
The eyes of the soul can then light up--
As Christ's Spirit enters - to strengthen - to sup!

Why then be miserable, gloomy, or forlorn?*
Why be unhappy each day, hateful, so borne?*
Nay, but be happy - give joy - give glee!
For Christ came to awaken in you and in me,
Happiness, allowing our misery to flee!

So friend, be free, be happy, smile, and glow!
For Christ's happiness within
A glowing countenance will show!

You can be happy - you can be free!
Life can count for something--
For Jesus can live in YOU!
And in me!

Lorna Sparks Gutierrez

Inspirational Verse
John 10:10 (KJV)
(Jesus said) "....I am come that they might have life and have it more abundantly."

* Negative emotions speak of heavy burdens, which many have borne (carried). Jesus said He would share our burdens!
Matthew 11:28 (NIV) "Come to me, all you who are weary and burdened, and I will give you rest!"
Then He stated that His burden is light (easy to carry). We all need Someone with whom we can share our burdens!

Why This Fighting?

What is all this fighting between human races?
Is color the only problem that Prejudice faces?
I've seen white men contentious with white--
And black with black, one upon one, fight.

And brown with brown, fighting too easy.
All fighting is stupid - just between you and me.
The problem is deeper it seems - than mere men.
It appears the problem is old-fashioned Sin!

I know the answer, but do you know it?
And if you did, would you have the fortitude to show it?
We all know Christ came to save us from sin.
Now, men can now go free - with Power to amend.
Wrong is wrong, and right is right;
And, between and in between our races - we should not fight!

I know a black lady, who has no color with me.
And I've no color with her, for in us both, Christ we see.
I see Christ in her; she sees Christ in me.
That's why we feel okay together, and we are then both free!

When we sit at Jesus' feet, there is no Prejudice there.
All is Beauty - all is Love - because God's Spirit fares.
Hand in hand, we all shall fly to that Yonder Land--
Where Christ's Spirit in Heaven dwells along with Peaceful Man.

If I give my heart to Jesus - and you give yours to Jesus too,
There is nothing great that we can't accomplish together.
In my heart, I know that's true!

Lorna Sparks Gutierrez

Inspirational Verse
Luke 1:37 (KJV)
For with God nothing shall be impossible.

Wondering - Wandering?

We think we're lost - we think we're alone.
We look for Peace - and look for Home.

We need to look UP - and then around,
So we can see where to be found.

And when we see - we will see Christ.
His Holy Spirit will suffice.

For with God we are never alone--
And thru Jesus our God, our sins are atoned.

Jesus our Lord paid the cost,
So that we never have to be lost.

In Christ we have an Eternal Friend--
And in Christ, an Eternal Home - now as then!

No more to wonder, no more to roam--
For Jesus IS our Peace, our Home!

Lorna Sparks Gutierrez

Inspirational Verse
John 14:6 (KJV)
(Jesus said) "I am the Way, the Truth, and the Life: No man cometh unto the Father, but by Me."

Worshipping The Three-Inch "god"

A problem?
Oh, don't tell me about 'im! He's mine you see!
And taking him before others is my prerogative!
Others say he makes me sick and makes me poor;
But I continue to love him - more and more!
Everyday I don't have him, I am just driven mad;
Even to the point of anger - it's so sad, sad, sad!
Around my friends I hear them say,
"You haven't quit YET?" - I hear it all day;
I begin to wonder why some from me shy away!

I have a chronic cough, and my children are always sick.
Why, it couldn't be MY fault for I'm really very slick!
My clothes have a distinct odor and aire; at times, I can't get my breath!
My quitter friends tell me this habit could result in misery and death!
Why, don't they know THAT won't happen to ME?
Why, I am so happy, can't they all see?
I ask myself where I mislaid my little stick god,
As I glance down at fingernails yellowing like ancient sod!
Could it be nicotine which causes my nails to appear yellow?
You know, it is for sure I've spent a lot of money on these inchy fellows.

I could have spent it on relaxing vacations,
Or traveled over Earth thru ten or twenty nations!
But I chose, as choices go, to purchase this adult pacifier.
However, at least, to others I am not a liar.......

A conscience:
But to myself? .... (*Yes, this one lies to himself*)--
My friends imply I have no common sense;
To them it is apparent I have become just dense.
Could they be right that I panic when he is not in sight?
It seems my hands begin to shake and my eyes over-glaze;
And I lose my mind when I breath in smoky haze!

It seems this lifeless three-inch god means more, you see,
Than obeying the God who created me.
I know I should not smoke, but to stop - I say, "I can't".
Oh, and you must be quiet for you know I will just rant!

Advice:
But the Lord does not excuse one's choice to self-abuse!
The three-inch god cannot give you life;
You give him the power to give you poverty and strife.
Now for which god are you willing to choose?
For with One you win - and with the other you will lose!
Which will YOU choose?

Lorna Sparks Gutierrez

Inspirational Verses
John 10:10 (NKJV) "I am come that they might have life, and that they might have it more abundantly."
Joshua 24:15 (NKJV) "....... And if it SEEM EVIL unto you to serve the LORD, choose you this day whom ye WILL serve; whether the gods which your fathers served or......:but as for me and my house, we will serve the Lord."
2 Corinthians 7:1(NKJV) " Having therefore these promises, dearly beloved, let us cleanse ourselves from all filthiness of flesh and spirit, perfecting holiness in the fear of God!"
2 Timothy 1:7 (NKJV) "For God has not given us the spirit of fear; but of Power, and of Love, and of a Sound Mind"!
Phillipians 4:13 (NKJV)" I can do all things through Christ who strengthens me!"
YOU GOT THE POWER!!!

Family

Friends

Related Poetry

D. Family and Friends Related Poetry

Dearest Dad
(A Father's Day Note)

Every day we honor you!
But this special day is yours, too!
We'll be glad when you are home.
We want you here, ne'er more to roam!

You have a special place in our hearts--
A special place no one can share in part!
So please, we hope to see you soon with us--
For, we've got a lot of things to discuss!

We're excited as can be to know you'll soon be near--
Our hearts will be full of happiness and cheer!
We need you Dad, to guide our steps and our ways--
To help direct our future and our present today!

You even mean so much to mom--
And she really misses you.
But no less Dad--
WE really miss you too!

Hurry home soon!
Hip-hip-hooray!
From all of us kids--
HAPPY FATHER'S DAY!

Lorna Sparks Gutierrez

Inspirational Verse
Ephesians 6: 1-4 (KJV)
Children, obey your parents in the Lord, for this is right. 2. "Honor your father and mother", which is the first
commandment with promise, 3. that it may be well with you and you may live long on earth. 4. and you, fathers, do
not provoke your children to wrath, but bring them up in the training and admonition of the Lord.

Loving Advice From Mom

My dear sweet child, remember me--
The mother of your heart!
I am but a flashing spirit--
Just here for your life to cheer it!

Take heed not to detest
The one who surely has loved you her best!
Don't misunderstand when advice has been handed--
For no criticism is meant, nor meanness demanded!

All is spent in work, in talk, for your best--
And nothing has been spoken in lightness nor jest!
From your birth until my death, remember I've loved you--
I've loved you.....my best!

Lorna Sparks Gutierrez

My Dad

I remember Daddy, quiet and strong!
He was thoughtful and religious--
And tried to do no wrong!
Daddy helped me have a conscience--
He spanked me when I was bad!
Those stern knowing looks he gave me,
Made me think I'd be quite sad!
Then he'd smile and give me comfort,
And help me along the way.
And, his quiet and timely advice
Gave me strength to go on each day.
I hope I made him proud of me--
That he'd be proud today!
I hope he'd know I have sweetest memories--
Daddy, in my heart you'll stay!

Lorna Sparks Gutierrez

My Friend Doris

I had a sweet friend named Doris.
She was a dear, sweet chum!
We walked a while in this world together;
Learning, growing, and having fun.

I played with her children;
I enjoyed running with her!
There was poetry, good books, and plays;
So much we shared - so rich we learned!

I received my diploma, and Doris did too!
My degree was in Science - Doris' in the Arts.
Often knowledge we gave the world that we could;
Then, Fate demanded that our paths part!

We stayed in contact as good friends ought
With occasional letters, calls, visits, and in thought.
I thank God for the moments we shared.
I do not forget how in friendship she cared!

One day God decided to take her.
He wanted her home with Him!
I cried and prayed, then had to settle that He had been kind
To let us share friendship for just a short time!

I keep her pictures, cards, and letters and reread them now and then;
And, think of all the good times, and how her friendship I did win!
Someday I'll see her in Heaven; for I KNOW that she is there!
I'll always think the world of her - I'm glad I showed Doris I cared!

Lorna Sparks Gutierrez

In Memory Of A Fine Friend, Doris Inez Steele

My Girls

Dona do Little and Tisha do Tiny,
Together those girls could be really quite whiny!
They'd say, "Do I have to do this?" or
"Do I have to do that?"
And, I'd flinch as I'd think to myself--
"Which can be the worse brat?!"

Then Tisha would do something sweet--
Like bake me a cake.
Or Dona would draw me a pretty picture--
My breath they'd both take!

Those girls I know I love them,
As on those sisters I'd ponder--
Without them the world would be poorer;
But with them I'm rich - I've no need to wonder!

Lorna Sparks Gutierrez

My Mom Is A Sweetheart

"I've the best!" - I've heard people say!
And I'll agree - me too - "Hooray!"
Not everyone has a good mother to love.
I know it's true she's a gift from above!

Love your mom, people, if you have one.
Not everyone is so lucky, you know, daughter or son.
Mother's are so easy to find fault with;
But to be respectful is a heavenly gift!

Respect your mom even when it's hard;
And on her birthday, send her a gift or card.
Moms aren't perfect, but really, who is?
But God gives what we need, so daughter, forgive!

You yourself may be a mother someday--
And raising children is hard, and rough, the way.
Mistakes are made, and prices paid.
To sculpture and influence souls,
Thereby, these personalities are made!

Some mothers are good, others aren't so kind!
But ALL will stand before the Lord in due time!
Mine has been great, she taught me about the Lord--
That Jesus saw all I did; and sin, I could not afford!

She and dad are the reason I'm a Christian today;
Besides, of the Lord's witness, I say!
My mom is certainly blest of Christ--
She's been instrumental in my Christian life!

Lorna Sparks Gutierrez

My Mother Is My Friend

My mother is my friend--
I want you to know.
She has been since I can remember,
And as I onward go.

My mother is my friend--
I want you to see
All the beautiful things
That she means to me!

My mother is my friend--
I want you to feel
The admiration I have for her;
It's true and it's real!

My mother is my friend--
I want you to hear
Of all the years she cared for me--
In her heart she kept me near.

My mother is my friend--
Whenever I was in need,
She provided the best for me--
A real friend indeed!

My mother is my friend--
For whenever I was ill,
Her love would warm me,
And chase away the chill!

My mother is my friend--
And I hope that I am hers!
I hope that I grow in her likeness,
With love that forever endures!

Lorna Sparks Gutierrez

My Mother's Guidance

When I was young, my heroine took care of me!
Whenever I was ill, she cared, she loved, you see!
She'd rock me to sleep, and sing me songs.
She'd quote little ditties and poems so long!

Mom would braid my hair and curl my tresses.
She'd wash my face and iron my dresses.
I admired her character, strong and good;
For what was best and right, she stood!

When I was bad, she'd scold, and to me she would tell-
That if I wanted to be bad, that there really was a Hell!
The Bible stated so, and she'd read that Book to me;
And tell of Jesus' Love, how He died to set men free!

She said the angels saw ALL I did--
That Jesus loved me, and sin was "forbid"!--
That I'd be happier if I made my Maker my friend--
So I did, for I saw in that God, His love she did lend!

She was kind, and generous, an example she set.
If anything went wrong, over us, she'd fret.
She was human, I'm glad, for who of us is not?--
But, she tried to please the Lord as best she thought!

She is my mother - Georgia - is her name.
If there is a Book of Mothers, I know she's in great fame!
I'm glad the Lord chose her for me.
Love your mom too, people, while there is time; you will see!

And if you don't have a mother, adopt you a good friend.
Treat her kindly until life's end.
As you see, there are plenty of good moms to be had.
Choose one for yourself; you'll both be glad!

And remember, dear woman, if you be a mother,
Life is short; don't let burdens be a bother!
Overcome, as Christ told us to do.......
Let's enjoy our mothers - Let them enjoy us too!

Lorna Sparks Gutierrez

My Sons

Two gifts from God--
Two little brothers,
Now grown and manly,
I'm proud of them before others!

Not many mothers can say,
"I'm proud of my sons!"
But I'm grateful I can
Stand with other grateful ones!

The two serve the Lord
In each his own way.
I know God will bless them
Both richly each day!

I trust God for each son's future;
I trust God for each son's wife.
Of God's love, I know I can be sure
Will live gloriously in each son's life!

Lorna Sparks Gutierrez

141

My Sparkling Spankies

Her curls fly - she's an apple of my eye!
In his eyes are mischievous twinkles,
And in his grin, cutie-pie dimples!

Children are pearls in the sands of life--
They need a little polish
To shine in the light!

Each is a pearl,
A jewel on the beach of beauty.
Love shining them up,
Each has meaning by duty!

I'll have more to bless my heart
This era faring;
We'll learn and grow together
In loving and sharing!

Pet names I'll call each,
And I'll have more
To bless my heart, Sparkling Spankies,
As *GRANDCHILDREN* walk into my door!

Lorna Sparks Gutierrez

Ode to Joyce

As we, on the playground, were standing together,
I heard someone mutter, "Hey, Mutt and Jeff", (remember them?)
My eyes got big, but you just smiled, and gave a sly grin!

Me, so short and you, so tall - (lucky you!), but that was the call!
We played, learned, and made good friends;
And, did the best we knew way back then!

You were tall and blonde, very kind and true!
And all the boys idolized you--
You were a true Best All Around, and popular too!

You had ambition, and so did I.
Hopes for our futures were mighty high.
We've overcome obstacles and tackled fears;
We've accomplished a lot over the years!

So congratulations, dear Birthday Girl!
Enjoy this Milestone, let it be a Thrill!
Life has just begun - there is more to do;
And YOU are just the one to do it--
You know that is so true!

God Bless you, Happy Birthday
Your friend,
Lorna Sparks Gutierrez
8/30/2015

This poem was written for Joyce Rowell for her birthday-September the 19th.

143

Ode to Tahni Sky

When news came around
That you were to be born,
Excitement exploded the air,
And lit the sky like the morn!

You were an answer to prayer
For a mom who prayed.
Your birth was on time;
It was not delayed.

But, before you were born
Grandma put in a request
When she saw an angel's picture--
Can you guess the rest?

'Twas that you'd be a chubby cherub
With blue eyes so rare,
With little coral cheeks,
And golden, curly hair!--

With the strength of an Amazon,
And tall to boot!--
And, the smile you gave,
You were just too cute!--

And like an angel--
A heart of gold--
With angelic characteristics--
A personality quiet, yet bold!

So, to Grandma you're an Angel--
And to your mom, a best friend...so rare!
And, to the world you'll be an answer;
Because, from God you came to care!

Lorna Sparks Gutierrez

Rachel's Friend
(And our Friend too)

Life is full of expectations--
Life is full of dreams--
Life is full of problems
And challenges it seems!

Sometimes problems surround us,
Standing in the way of success;
But, there is a Friend Who will guide you,
Who will stand between you and duress!

Sometimes we need a Hero,
Who will help us conquer our fears--
Who will hold our hand to guide us
Thru out the coming years.

A Friend will give you faith to conquer,
And give you faith to succeed--
A Friend where, when, there is none,
He can fulfill every need!

A personal Friend is One Who will love you,
When no one else is around.
He'll protect, comfort, and guide you
Thru out life - from sun-up to sun-down!

I have found that He has helped me,
As He will surely aid you!
By just asking Him, He'll be there--
With Him life can be brand-new!

He will keep His promises;
What He says - He WILL do!
Since you are special to JESUS,
The Lord will be special to you!

Lorna Sparks Gutierrez

Inspirational Verses
John 15:13-17 (KJV)
Jesus said, "Greater love hath no man than this, that a man lay down his life for his friends.
(14) Ye are my friends, if ye do whatsoever I command you.
(15) Henceforth I call you not servants.....but I have called you friends ...
(16) Ye have not chosen me, but I have chosen you ...
(17) These things I command you, that you love one another."
Written for a friend, Rachel D., Annemarie's daughter.

To Camille Joy

There are many children, who may attest,
That their start in life was not the best!
The reasons are many and not few;
But, to avoid lasting effects, what should one do?

First, study and learn all you are able.
Do all you can to make your life stable.
So, not to be weak, take the Lord by His hand.
He'll give you the advice your life needs to understand--

That the Lord has an expected end for you!*
So take His Hand - so it all can come true!
His Light will shine upon your path--
He'll bless your way - and all that you ask!

So Granddaughter, with eyes of hazel blue-green,
The Lord really says what He means!
The Lord's Spirit is here to show you what to do--
No matter if your eyes were black, brown, or blue!

He is the Good Father that many children never have!
And for hurts and wounds, He has the healing salve!
The Lord will give you the faith it takes to succeed--
For all you have to do is ask Him!
His Spirit is eager to help you to believe!

Lorna Sparks Gutierrez

Inspirational Verses
Psalm 37:4 (NKJV)
Delight yourself also in the Lord, and He shall give you the desires of your heart.
Jeremiah 29:11-13 New King James Version (NKJV)
11 For I know the thoughts that I think toward you, says the Lord, thoughts of peace and not of evil, to give you a future and a hope. 12 Then you will call upon Me and go and pray to Me, and I will listen to you. 13 And you will seek Me and find Me, when you search for Me with all your heart.

*Jeremiah 29:11 (KJV)
King James Version says:
"For I know the thoughts that I think toward you, saith the Lord, thoughts of peace and not of evil, to give you an expected end."

To My Aunties

There are special people called Aunties,
And I know I have my share.
God blessed me with good ones:
Loving, sassy ladies who cared.

They blessed me with their kindness,
And showed me so much more:
Of rich beautiful stories
Of days lived years before!

I've heard how they picked cotton,
And rich yellow butter they made--
Of pretty hand-made dresses--
And entertaining suitors in the shade!

I've heard of sicknesses they lived over,
That would surely kill us nowadays--
Of struggles through hard times
That would make weaker people faint away!

Thank God for my Aunties
(Special people I love!)
For sharing their heritage with me--
And their blessings from God above!

Lorna Sparks Gutierrez

To My Daughter, Tisha

When I was six months pregnant, I began to get excited.
What if God gave me a daughter? I'd be pretty much delighted!
I couldn't understand why I hadn't wanted another baby.
Perhaps I didn't want it to suffer....but, this must be in God's plan, just maybe!
When you were born I couldn't believe my eyes!
Your beauty was outstanding, it would not be disguised!
Your slender, long fingers told me you'd play music, piano, or guitar.
And your hair, the angels curled, would open eyes and make mouths go ajar!
Those eyelashes that hit the back of your eyelids! Oh my!
"Not many could compare", in pride, I'd say and sigh!
You were too skinny, but I'd take care of that.
Too skinny is unhealthy, I'd see you'd get some fat.
You were so lovely; I'd just sit and stare.
God had given us a beauty, outstanding and so fair!
I know I'd love you as I held you to my heart.
I prayed nothing in this world would ever tear our love apart.
As you were 1, you'd walk and smile and sing.
As you were 2, you'd talk and climb high on the swing.
As you were 3, you'd even make your own bed.
As you were 4, tie your older brothers' shoes (yes, that's what I said).
At 5, you were smart and wanted to go to school;
But had to wait 'til you were 6, 'cause it was the rule.
At 6 you started kindergarten; I hated to see you go!
But you were a "big girl" now, well - so-so!
And at 7, you were in 1st grade, so mature!
And at 8 you prayed for a sister, God answered you that year!
At 9, you took piano lessons, you were very good!
I'd smile to myself in pride as you played, God understood.
At 10, you helped me baby-sit, you could be trusted.
At 11, you wanted to wear make-up, a little didn't hurt; you mussed it.
And at 12, you got rebellious, the "age thing" they say.
At 13, you shocked me by your hardness that way!
You hated your hair - you hated your weight.
But we both know there is help for everything - it's never "too late"!
At 14, you took an interest in the boys.
You seemed to put aside your girlish toys.
At 15, you seemed to have a bundle of friends.
Their comings and goings seemed never to end!
At 16, we collided, over growing pains and problems so tall!
But as did then, 'twill now - love conquers all!
Now you are 17, the future is yours - simply plan it.
See what you want to be; follow thru! Claim it!
You can be what you want; dream it and it shall be!--
Because I KNOW you were born for a reason - it's destiny!
God has a plan for the rest of your life.
Just follow the Lord - He can handle ANY strife!
If you take hold of God's hand, you'll never walk alone.
The rest of your years can be beautiful; "Tisha music" will set the tone.
You'll make life richer for others, and they'll be glad you were born.
Your strength of soul and toughness will heal other lives that've been torn.
I hope by this poem that you can see only a mite of my heart.
It's full of love for you Tisha, but only you see a part.
For my love for you is much, if you could only know;
I believe in you Tisha! 'Tis upward and far you'll go!

Lorna Sparks Gutierrez

To My Daughter, Teniele

Right now it seems that you're so small,
That big brothers and sisters don't want you at all!
They think your ears might be too big--
That you'll hear something and tell it, you dig?

Oh, you're just too small to understand their conversation!
Oh, you might retell it! Oh dear, maybe in exact recitation!
Perhaps they might have to look after you, and then they'd be in a bind;
They'd rather feel free of responsibility than to be so confined!

Someday when you're older, they'll be a bit ashamed.
They'll look back upon these years in a little of disdain.
They'll wish they'd been more kinder, more patient, more smart--
That they could have you closer, more dear entwined in each heart!

So who has now more wisdom, them - or you - my dear?
Just cheer up to think you'll be one up in a few years!
They'll secretly be proud of their little sister who's big and grown!
Hopefully, your heart can forgive the immature treatment it has been shown!

But remember sweet child - once they were little too.
And if I could relive it, I'd be kinder to them too!
It seems we all grow wiser with each year that passes by;
We'll all look back and remember as tears drop from our eyes!

But since we have the wisdom, let us love well while we can!
We can make our memories much sweeter with patient love to understand!

Lorna Sparks Gutierrez

(Note from eldest sister)
Sissy, you've grown into a beautiful, intelligent, fine young woman.
And I couldn't be more proud of you than I already am.
And it's no secret at all! You truly are my hero!
I admire you more than words could ever express.
In my book, you truly are the best!

Treasures to Remember

Their little church and school mementos - little treasured things they made,
I kept in a box and large gift sack - offerings of love to me they gave.
There under my bed and in the closet on a crest-like shelf,
Were treasures that brought tears to my eyes and joy to myself.

There had gotten to be so many!
At times I took them out and put them in a pile,
To give some back to them in remembrance,
Of things each one had done as a child.

The memories had opened their eyes of the moment,
Bringing a thought of nostalgic gladness to them--
Of a joyous moment in time - to be treasured once again!

You know, I still keep a few to remind me;
I need to be reminded every once in a while!
I know one day they will take these out to examine,
To remember good times with a smile!

Then they will know that once I am gone,
That I loved and thought of them all - everyone!
Memories of love forever to be shared,
Treasured in my heart - to show how I cared!

Lorna Sparks Gutierrez

You Too May Someday Be Old

….And then my Mother said to me, as she began to scold,
That I, too, might someday "be old"!
I hung my head (but unashamedly), for I
Did not want to tell my Grandmother ANY sweet goodbye!

I thought her to be hateful; her demeanor was just so strict!--
For I was spoiled, 'twas true, and I was "pretty slick"!

She probably had my "number" (what a bummer!)--
For I was a haughty 5 year-old, and not a "little" BOLD!

….And I was not one bit shy, as I began to think and sigh,
That she might just be a little mean--
(Why, you'd have thought I was Grandchild # 13)!

With a little sense of humor, as to how it was back then,
She was probably tired of all those spoiled grandchildren,
No matter had I been #2 or # 10!

So for all of us grandparents, altho I now understand,
That we're all as human as the grandkids, all-human, all of Man!

But this I must say: a little love and kindness will go a long-long way!
It would implant upon a child's mind, a better memory of any "someday".

Now remember............someday, you too, may "be old".
Perhaps you will remember what my mother to me told!

Lorna Sparks Gutierrez

Inspirational Verses for "You Too May Someday Be Old"

For Grandparents and Any Caregivers:

Ephesians 4:32 (NKJV)
"And be KIND to one another, tender-hearted, forgiving one another, even as God in Christ forgave you."
Proverbs 25:11 (NKJV)
"A word fitly spoken is like apples of gold in settings of silver."
Proverbs 22:6
"Train up a child in the way he should go, and when he is old he will not depart from it."

For Children and those who are in instructional care by others:

Proverbs 1:8 (NKJV)
"My son, hear the instruction of your father, and do not forsake the law of thy mother."
Proverbs 2:6 (NKJV)
"For the Lord gives wisdom; From His mouth comes knowledge and understanding."
Proverbs 3:11-12 (NKJV)
"My son, do not despise the chastening of the Lord, nor detest His correction:
(12) for whom the Lord loves He corrects, just as a father (corrects) the son in whom he delights."
Proverbs 12:1 (NKJV)
"Whoever loves instruction loves knowledge, but he who hates correction is stupid."
Proverbs 13:1 (NKJV)
"A wise son heeds his father's instruction, but a scoffer does not listen to rebuke."
Proverbs 15:31-33 (NKJV)
"The ear that hears the rebukes of life will abide among the wise." (32) "He who disdains instruction despises his own soul. But he who heeds rebuke gets understanding." (33) "The fear of the Lord is the instruction of wisdom. And before honor is humility."

Slightly

Humorous

Poetry

E. Slightly Humorous Poetry

A Good Trip

I'd love to go to Scotland
To watch the Keltics dance--
And after a stint in Ireland,
I'd shuffle to the South of France!

I'd perch on a heightened balcony
To gaze at city lights--
And sip fine tea by fireside
As I savor new delights!

I'd try the latest fashions--
Dare I dare! Or dare I don't?
And in my thoughts would I purchase?--
As money would be no point!*

I'd kiss the heads of little children,
And hug the sweet old ladies fair--
Maybe wink at a few good men!
And, then return solo to my own lair--

To contemplate of travels far,
Of running my feet thru sand,
Of swimming in coastal oceans,
And safari-ing on scenic lands.

Right now I live in Vegas--
To envy me, some might!
But even in "Vacation City",
A body could use a different sight!

But today is an adventure,
As I travel these anxious streets.
I'm sure to find excitement,
As I seek out new retreats.

Certainly, I'll pray God's watch-care--
For, this world has always been
Backslidden and resentful--
So full of wicked sin!

Someday when I get to Heaven,
There is there no Desert heat!
And I'll never have to leave it--
For Heaven's guaranteed to treat!

The Lord is there to greet me--
I won't have to fear those streets!
And, I'm sure to find new adventures
In Heaven's Great Retreat!

Lorna Sparks Gutierrez

* Remember, this poem is just a dream-money is always a point somewhere!-LOL!
P.S. I would want to visit England, Greece, and Italy too! I have already been to Mexico.
Isn't it amazing that God is Everywhere? He can even enter your heart!

Bills

I hope that tomorrow I'll get it all done--
But today they seem to be a son-of-a-gun!

The bills are piled high; I'll get to them when I can--
But today isn't in it; it's hard to fit them to plan!

One day at a time - but do the creditors know?
My budget is extended as far as it can go!

My only consolation - I'm not completely by myself!
Compared to other's debts, I'm a financial, tiny elf!

So I guess I'll just count blessings today--
As I deliberate tomorrow - then, the bills I'll pay!

Lorna Sparks Gutierrez

Inspirational Verse
Romans 13:8 (KJV)
"Owe no man anything, but to love one another, for he that loveth another hath fulfilled the law."

But That Doesn't Just Happen In Your Teens!

Growing up is so hard, it's true!
The Journey is rough - or so it seems.
Why even the one you love doesn't love you!
BUT THAT DOESN'T JUST HAPPEN IN YOUR TEENS!

It seems the zits, they start to show--
The figure you got doesn't fit your dreams!
Your hairstyle isn't the desired curl or glow,
BUT THAT DOESN'T JUST HAPPEN IN YOUR TEENS!

The response to the question, "Will you go out with me?"
Might be "Ugh, no" (or would that RSVP be too mean?)
Instead, guess I'll ponder "Hmmm!" or "Yippee!"
BUT THAT DOESN'T JUST HAPPEN IN YOUR TEENS!

Confidence grows with oncoming years.
Thank God for that - And on Him one leans.
There's gratefulness of experience and recovery of tears--
BUT THAT DOESN'T JUST HAPPEN IN YOUR TEENS!

Lorna Sparks Gutierrez

Can Anyone Have A Frankenstein In Him?

Every man is put together with many different parts.
There is the good, the bad, the bright, and the sad.
…And for this poem to rhyme, we must consider Frankenstein!

Does everyman have a little of him?
Can a man control that part that would have him sin?
Can a man control his monster inside?
That monster called Temper can take you for a ride!

A Temper can make you a real Frankenstein,
Unless you lock him up in the jail of your mind!
Let Good reign in the stronghold of your mind--
Be strong and keep Temper Frankenstein in line!

You are only in control when you hold the Key!
So don't let 'Ole Franken' out for all the world to see!
Remember anyone can have little Frankensteins,
But, we all must be in control - so we don't lose our minds!

P.S. If you don't have a key - get one.
If you do have a key - don't lose it! Ha-ha-ha!
My key is the Bible!

Lorna Sparks Gutierrez

Note: This poem was written for Tahni Douzat, my Granddaughter, to help her with a school project.

If I Had a Million

If I had a million, what would I do?

Would I act crazy like a monkey in a zoo?

Or would I be sensible and sit down to think?

Put down a budget to dream on paper and ink?

Would I have room in my budget for love and goodwill?

Pay all my bills and save for a well-deserved thrill?

WELL--

Only GOD knows what I would do!

(Now I think I will just consult Him), wouldn't you?

Lorna Sparks Gutierrez

It's Math....It's Math!

It's math....it's math
So let us be unscathed.

It's just a game
To tease one's brain.

If you like crosswords and neo-genesis*,
Don't allow math to be a negative nemesis!

Play the game; just go by the rules--
You'll come out shining with new skill tools!

And simply remember--
It's only a game**--
To tease one's brain!

Lorna Sparks Gutierrez

Inspirational Verses

2 Timothy 2:15 (KJV)
"Study to show thyself approved unto God, a workman that needeth not to be ashamed, rightly dividing the word of truth."

Isaiah 41:13 (KJV)
"For I, the Lord thy God, will hold thy right hand, saying unto thee, 'Fear not; I will help thee.'"!

*Neogenesis (new beginnings),
**A very important, functional game!

Merry Christmas All Dieters!

Cinnamon sticks - and Peppermint patties!
Here's a Holiday Cheer for all of us fatties!

Red Holly Berries and Green Holly Wreaths!
Now all of us dieters - let's not be cheats!

Fat around the fanny - or thick in the middle--
We're told we must be "Fit as a fiddle!"

So - get out your pencil or get out your pen
To write down this resolution - "We must be thin!"?

Maybe Old Saint Nick will leave us a present
Of "Determination on a Diet", that just might be pleasant!

I'm really all for it - I want to be thin--
As a twinkle's in my eye, and I give you a grin!

Ho - Ho - Ho!
Merry Christmas!

Lorna Sparks Gutierrez

Mother's Manual

"How does it feel to be a mother?" I thought.
As I heard her say to her kids,
"Now....get in this car NOW!"
(Children don't come with a "mother's manual" to show you "how")

No matter how good you were to the brood,
Some might think you were *TOO* good!
I laughed, for I knew one thing,
That there are those who would think you mean!

And no matter how much you loved the bunch--
To sacrifice loads each day,
It would seem ungratefulness would spring its ugly head--
To surprise you - and find fault, I say!

A touch of humor, a grain of salt to the skill--
You'll find, will sweeten the burden, and will
Warm the heart, and give heart to the soul,
And make lighter the days, as older you grow.

Don't let it be too much, just stand--
And do your best, asking God's wisdom and man's.
And, realize you *ARE* fit for this job--
As good as any mother's tears she's sobbed!

But laugh and giggle for it's not all tears!
And smiles will grow throughout the years!
With discipline, love, humor, and a grin--
Here's hoping for you it turns out well in the end!

Lorna Sparks Gutierrez

Inspirational Verse:
Proverbs 22:6 (KJV)
"Train up a child in the way he should go, and when he is old he will not depart from it."

The Heartfelt Angel

An Angel, resting on a golden-tipped wing,
Began to strum a heart, as a song the angel did sing!

Angel eyes scanned the heavens, as cottony clouds danced by.
And, not a single thing could pass those eagle-lit eyes!

The human below wondered why his heart began to sing--
As cheeriness stirred within him, the clouds had a silver gleam!
Did he hear a laugh? Or was it just a dream?

The Angel smiled, lifted, and eyed another needed place.
The Angel would give another hungry soul laughter and good grace!

There was business at hand, and a joy it was!
Spreading cheer thru the heavens,
And thru the earth.......LOVE!

Lorna Sparks Gutierrez

163

The Pumpkin Moon

The amber pumpkin moon caught my eye,
As it slowly slid across an autumn, October sky.

Dark yellow as cheese and round as a ball,
Its magic seemed to enthrall us all!

Its craters appeared - from earth - as a mouth and two eyes.
The moon looked eerie - and a little too wise!

Formations of clouds gave an eerie sight,
As the clouds tailed grey in the chilly, bite-y night.

A good moon for an October-Harvest night,
Would set people telling those stories of fright!

I told myself not to be afraid of the moon's mystic call--
For it really - is only - a moon….after all!

Lorna Sparks Gutierrez

The Season

Pumpkin is good,
Pumpkin is great,
Whether it be in the form
Of a cookie or a cake.

Take a bite
And give a grin!
Lick up that icing
On your tongue or chin!

Enjoy the Season
And all the LOVE it brings,
With sugary spice
And savory things!

Lorna Sparks Gutierrez

165

Too Particular!

(Particular Husband Speaking)

The dinner doesn't look so good; I'll have to check on that!
If I don't think I'll like it, I'll just give 'em a verbal attack!
My steak is too thick - or is it just too thin?
You know, if it's not a name brand, then it HAS to be a SIN!

You KNOW I don't like this - not EVEN a version of that!
It could make me skinny - or it just might make me FAT!
Well, I KNOW it won't taste good - why, it COULDN'T, you see!
Surely I'll have to GRADE it - only F's, and D's or C's!

Well, perhaps I should take her advice--
And maybe just brush my teeth?
She said I might smell my food right, and
REALLY taste that beef!

She said if I don't like it - "Then, just go out to eat!"
She said she'd take a long vacation,
And hire someone else to take this 'heat'!

Lorna Sparks Gutierrez

By: Mariah G.

'Twixt and 'Tween

Wouldn't it be nice to come out of yourself--
To hang one's body on a top notch shelf?

Your body could rest and relax it's true;
And, your spirit could soar and spy and sleuth!

Ah, let's be selfish,
Lest some spirit see
Our body resting, and want it - maybe!

So you keep what's yours, and
I'll keep what's mine--

And together, we'll both be
Fine, fine, fine!

Lorna Sparks Gutierrez

The Big Thrilling Ride

Now what could I do and what could I say,
To assure he'd be careful as he rode away?
He was going to do it; be sure that he would!
As he was that way - to do all that he could!

He had donned on the helmet and donned on the gloves--
And had jumped to the seat to do all that he loves!
He flipped on the switch and gave it the gas
To rev up his scooter with a smile--could it last?

He backed out of the driveway and gave it some more.
He flew down the street, giving distance from his door.
The wind flew wildly thru his hair - the smile grew greater,
As he distanced his care!

Oops! He forgot to slow down as he stepped on the brakes--
He did not want to wreck or die, for Heaven's sake!
He hit a bump and flew to the side!
And.... that was the end of his exciting ride!

He got up and was glad he could!
And later he would think it over, as he should!
Lucky and blest was he to be alive--
Was he less broken than the vehicle he did drive?

One must be careful; it is hard when one is young--
For some people might think that "careless" could be fun!
And.... it is well to be concerned--
For that is life - it is lessons learned!

Lorna Sparks Gutierrez

Written for her Grandson, Michael

Miscellaneous

Poetry

F. Miscellaneous Poetry

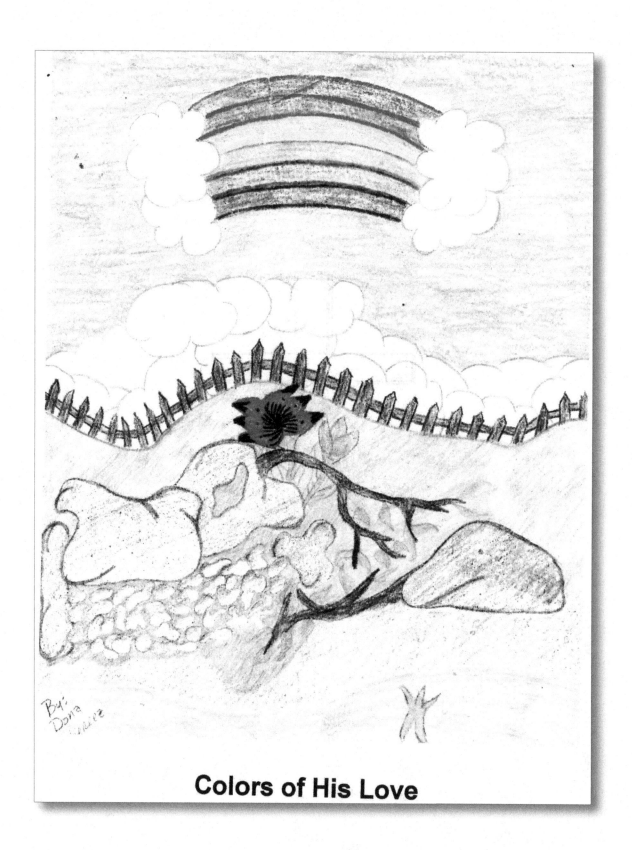

Colors of His Love

Colors of His Love

Born from inquiry into my mind,
I found a rainbow of colors sublime.
Their meaning, a rainbow from above;
It seemed to form the colors of Love.

Black is elegance supreme--
Life is ever in all of green--
White is purity and dilutes the rest--
Blue forms shades of cool restfulness.

Brown is ever an earthy tone--
Crème is blendable, a color not alone!
Purple is royalty; steely silver, might--
Gold, the color of richness and right--

Pink, the color of happy shades--
Red, the Life of Passion's rage--
Orange, the intelligence of reflection's rays--
Yellow, the gaiety of sunny days--

In ALL of them I found something to see.
Something - yes, inside of me!
A rainbow of life, a rainbow of above--
Look around you, people--
These are colors of His Love!

Lorna Sparks Gutierrez

Inspirational Verses

Genesis 9:13-14 (KJV)
I do set my bow (rainbow) in the cloud, and it shall be for a token of a covenant between me and the earth.
And it shall come to pass, when I bring a cloud over the earth, that the bow shall be seen in the cloud.

God Made Us To--

God made us to work--
God made us to play--
God made us to plan--
God made us to stay.

God made us to rest--
God made us to live--
God made us to task--
God made us to forgive.

God made us to be--
God made us to hear--
God made us to see--
God made us to fear.

God made us to feel--
God made us to know--
That God's love is REAL,
As we live and we grow!

Lorna Sparks Gutierrez

Inspirational Verses

Please read Genesis chapters 1 and 2 (KJV)
Also Jeremiah 29:11 (KJV)
"For I know the thoughts that I think toward you, saith the Lord, thoughts of peace, and not of evil, to give you an expected end."

Godly Shades Of Blue

The bluest blue near a midnight shade,
Just a shade in the eve at seven--
It's beauty relayed as shade on shade
*Formed an accolade, as I gazed towards the Heavens.

The city lights in the valley below
Gleamed, but looked so shallow!
In comparison to that shade of blue,
That blue made the lights look sallow!

Usually the lights look like diamonds bright
As they flicker, gold and white.
But man-made things, although they gleam,
Compared to God's creation, they just don't quite!**

No picture in blue I've seen before
Was as breathtaking as that BLUE!
It seemed to have a soul of its own,
As it shaded in circles around Heaven's throne!

I've heard that stones will even praise God--
That His creations praise His Name too!
For I saw God worshipped that silent night
In glorious, Godly shades of blue!

Lorna Sparks Gutierrez

Inspirational Verse

Psalm 8:1 (KJV)
"O, Lord our Lord, how excellent is thy Name in all the earth! who has set thy glory above the heavens."!

Note: an accolade is a mark of recognition or a symbol of praise or a salute, in this case, to God.

**They just don't quite compare.*

Gratefulness

Count your blessings instead of what is not.
Thank God for good already given, what you now have got.
Be glad for riches in your soul, and
Take glory for happy moments.

For life is not in what surrounds us.
Life is in the joy of our hearts,
The bubbling over of spirit and soul inside ourselves,
Reaching to God and flowing over to other souls,
Rejoicing them!

Lorna Sparks Gutierrez

In Getting It Done

If I should do nothing, I will believe this lie,
That Fate would be late,
If I should but procrastinate!

Fate WILL be on time, but will I be ready?
Only if I plan, and put to my hand
The plow, and steady work, hour by hour!

And to that mountain, a piece at a time,
It will remove, and diminish.
Then in readiness, I will see
My heart, filled with hope, replenished!

Perhaps the work would be more than just that;
But maybe give hope to another, in fact--

To another, who is just about to give up and out;
And would inspire that one to continue on and about!

That inspiration and glory awaits those who are zealous.
That will help them, as God is really for us!

So you and I must not give up hope;
The Lord is here to help us to cope.

And He will see that our work will get done,
From our birth to our death, with each rising sun!

Lorna Sparks Gutierrez

Inspirational Verse

Philippians 1:6 (NKJV)
St. Paul said, "...being confident of this very thing, that He that has begun a good work in you will complete it until the day of Jesus Christ!"

In Memory Of A Friend

A lapse of time and our paths do cross.
As dice of time, Fate does toss.
We meet it seems by accident,
When could be meant - by circumstance.

How long friendships can last, life's trials tell;
The strength of the bonds weakened by blows pell-mell.
Eventually broken by errors and sins,
Bonds can be made stronger - if mended again!

How bonds are mended, both parties must seek
For real repentance on both sides - (now don't cheat!)
For it takes BOTH parties to heal fractures and breaks--
And enormous love.... to overcome those human mistakes!

We can overcome Fate by our own sheer will
By loving and caring - doing God's bidding still.
We must while we can; Life is short it is true--
A "Vapor of Smoke"; *what is left is what we do*!

Lorna Sparks Gutierrez

My Boss!

I have felt God walk with me
In faith thru out eternity.
I know I must also walk with Him--
Anything less, for myself, would be a sin!

I've seen thru out my life,
Blessedness and Anxious Strife!
Thru out all these, He was in the Distance!
Altho I wondered where He was in MY existence!

However, I told Him,
"Do not let me go."
And in His Love, His Love He showed!
He showed up, and He showed off!*
'Twas then I knew He'd be my Boss!

Lorna Sparks Gutierrez

Inspirational Verse

Matthew 7:7 (NKJV)
"Ask and it will be given to you; Seek and you will find; Knock, and the door will be opened to you."

Jeremiah 29:13 (NKJV)
"And you will seek me and find me when you search for me with all your heart."

Ephesians 3:20 (AKJV) "Now unto Him that is able to do exceeding abundantly above all that we ask or think...."

*The Lord showed (off) to me, that he could give and love me more than I had ever asked or thought to have asked him for!

My Favorite Place

My feet taste the carpet green,
Where all is peaceful and serene--
Shades of red and blue in twilight,
It grows darker, bluer.... quiet.

I sit waiting for the calm
To engulf my soul in its balm--
A place my being will enfold,
As joy wells up inside my soul.

A quiet moment that calms encroaching fears--
That endears my heart and lightens the years.
Alone here with God, I'd rather stay--
The most precious moment of a long-awaited day!

Lorna Sparks Gutierrez

Ode To a CCU Nurse

This is a real cardiac affair,
Open only to nurses "Who Dare"!
Each hopes his or her patient is not in cardiac arrest,
As testimony of every CCU nurse can attest!

It's not hard to have your own PVC's,
When stress attacks as the monitor beeps!
Now the crash cart is ready - so's the atropine and dig--
Watch that monitor! - (please, no flutter or fib!)

Let's give these people credit - the credit is due.
These nurses are hard working, reliable, and true!
They deserve distinction and courtesy, every then and now--
As portraying their profession, they really show you "how"!

Now put yourself in their places - could you do so well?
Could you be so pleasant when frustration bombshells?
Would you have a sense of humor after some doc. makes his rounds?
(While he shouts orders as he slams his stethoscope down?)

Well, I'm proud of those nurses, I really must say--
These soldiers in white, we need them to stay!
Now let's honor their profession and give them a grin--
And thank God for them, again and again and again!

Lorna Sparks Gutierrez

Of Castles In The Air!

She stepped her foot upon the cobbled-stone floor,
Dancing down on steps so chill.
Her eyes searched hurriedly
For his image upon yon hill.

Her hair fell gracefully o'er her breast--
The babe snuggled warmly near her heart--
Above on the wall hung the Shalott crest--
As Elaine prayed, "Please Lancelot, ne'er more depart!"

But he of roving eye did have!
He was of the gallant and brave say they!
But not enough! For tortures in private fears did rave
For Elaine inside her head!

But the child was of great consequence,
For 'twas all she had of him!
And if never all his love she'd have,
At least in the child she'd win!

Even in death, the spirit would not still--
She'd think of Lancelot evermore--
And the castle where she and the child lived,
And that walk on the cold stone floor!

Then "Elaine" awoke from her regressive trance,
Happily estranged from that "other" life!
In her eyes, bittersweet memories danced,
Divorced from its madness and yearning strife!

Well, it may be nice to have lived before--
Or maybe, even to have known--
But, I'll take a walk on today's warm carpet
To a bare dance on life's cold stone floor!

And love is good, but love YOURSELF!--
For aren't dreams just castles in the air?
For even a little hut can be great,
If God's Peace and Trust abide there!

Lorna Sparks Gutierrez

Inspirational Verse

John 14:27 (KJV)
"Peace I leave with you, my peace I give unto you: not as the world gives, give I unto you."

Written for Florine Wells: A friend

187

Oh, The Hope of a Dream!

My days were weary, and oh, so dreary.
And then the dream was dreamed!
Envisioned was an ethereal child,
Who in Heaven had left her wings!

She smiled aglow with brightness fair,
And looked right straight my way.
I saw within her eyes, she might brighten any day!

"Oh," said I, "stay awhile, please, to cheer my heart,
Hopefully, long, and ne'er to depart--
A joy 'twould be, for anyone with you to know--
Your lovely persona would engagingly show!"

Then I awoke with a smile on my face
To think of this child, I would love to embrace--
To think of hopes to give to her
In exchange - for her loving allure!

The dream was so strange, but I envisioned to see
That someday there, a child could be waiting for me!
And in my heart, hope was my own--
That for the both of us - we would not be alone!
The dream was there for me to see--
Now I must wait in faith - the promise - patiently!

Lorna Sparks Gutierrez

Note:
There have been many women, who loved children and wanted one of their own, who can identify with this emotion.

Oh, Lullaby Baby

Lullaby Baby, when you are well,
Asleep with a grin - the angels won't tell!

They will guard you and guide you;
You mustn't peep!
They'll give you sweet dreams while you're asleep!

Lullaby Baby, when you are sick,
We will chase those gremlins away very quick!
Fevers will break - that, the angels will take!
And in sweet dreams you will slumber
To be well when awake!

Lullaby Baby, hold you in my arms--
To see your sweet face and take in all your charms!
Lullaby Baby, Sweet Baby so fine,
I would love you even if you weren't mine!

Oh Lullaby Baby, as I caress your cheek,
Your warmness surrounds me in clouds of "so sweet"!
And a place in my heart there'll always be,
For Sweet Lullaby Baby, asleep on my knees!

Lorna Sparks Gutierrez

Inspirational Verses

Luke 18: 16-17 (NKJV)
(Jesus said)
"Allow the little children to come unto me, and forbid them not: for of such is the kingdom of heaven."
"Verily, I say unto you, Whosoever shall not receive the kingdom of God as a little child shall in no wise enter therein."

On Parents

I guess there's no one I love better
Than my mom - except my dad, of course!
Apparently I was lucky they didn't
Acquire the "Grande Divorce".

However and again, my children
Think a different thought these days.
They didn't have the parents I had--
Theirs were worse! Oh, thoughts of Dismay!

It's hard to be a parent--
We all know that is true!
But is it harder to be married,
Or have a case of old fashioned flu?

I wish I could have given my children better,
Had I been so smart or wise!
I wouldn't then bear any guilt or shame,
As thoughts of myself I once despised!

But thank God for forgiveness,
And a chance to start over again--
To be a better parent and companion,
And maybe someday, their friendship to win!

Lorna Sparks Gutierrez

(Note from daughter)
Mom, you always were, still are, and will always be my friend.
I love you so much, and will love you till life's end.
I know you ALWAYS did the best you could.
And sometimes we kids...well, we didn't act like we should.
The only thing I think you could have done better,
Was maybe get rid of the boys--
So you could buy me and the little sister more toys!
(Totally joking...only put that in there 'cause it rhymed...hahahaha)

On Talent

No matter how small you think it is--
Do not it ignore!
For even the greatest oak tree was born
From one small, hidden, dirty acorn!

The greatest diamond was not seen
At first upon a beautiful hand--
But, was first seen with greatest awe
In a dusty, deep mine or land!

Take that talent day by day,
Nurture to demand!
Give it love and encouragement--
Sift it through life's sand!

A thing of beauty you'll behold,
A thing of great delight!
If given love's attention, it
Will grow from small to might!

Lorna Sparks Gutierrez

Spring

Spring is a time of beginning,
A time to anew, fraught with hope--
After the death of the winter,
To bring our visions to view, in scope.

But now, Spring is ever before us,
In the form of Jesus, our Lord!
His Spirit is here to renew us;
He invigorates the stale, and brings life to the bored!

He adds vision to our blindness--
He strengthens the weak--
He adds color, life, harmony, and sunshine,
When all else would be bleak!

Jesus adds to the adventure,
And makes exciting the trip!
He's there to add to our comfort,
When we otherwise just might slip!

He's there, a Friend to the Friendless,
And Hope when all else would fail!
And He lightens the loads of the Weary,
And offers Friendship on any lonely, rough trail!

So renew yourself this Spring season!
--Or ANY time of the year!--
Just look in faith to The Savior,
Jesus the Lord, our Salvation so Dear!

Lorna Sparks Gutierrez

Thank You, Lord!

For giving me the strength to get thru--
For the small and large blessings daily
That put a smile on my face and heart--
For the peace that sometimes seems so far-reaching!--
For hope and vision over events that appear to be helpless--
For the passing compliment
That meant so little to someone else,
And SO much to me!--
For the smile that said, "It's nice to see you!"--
For inspiration to continue daily--
And for small kindnesses that were
Really very BIG to me at the moment!--
Thank You Lord!

Lorna Sparks Gutierrez

To Let Another Know

To show love is better than words--
To speak love is better than thought--
How else will another heart know,
If that love you do not show?

If love you give,
As it should be given,
'Twill make all the difference
For happiness in life and Heaven to envision!

For surely in turn
In some form or another,
That love will return to you, friend,
Parent, child, spouse, sister, or brother!

Boundaries there are
That one cannot cross.
And if respectful love is there,
Then there is no loss!

Love comes in many forms and ways:
Charitable, friendly, and even passionate displays!
But the best love one really knows,
Is the love that so fondly shows!

The day Christ died on Calvary,
God showed His love for you and me!
The Bible says God commendeth His love toward us,
That while we were yet sinners, Christ died for us.*

Therefore, I conclude and feel,
That the love that's shown is the love that's real.
In what we do and what we say,
We show God's love to one another each day!

Lorna Sparks Gutierrez

Inspirational Verse
*Romans 5:8 (KJV) states: "But God commendeth His love toward us, in that, while we were yet sinners, Christ died for us." The NKJV states: "God demonstrates His own love toward us......."

The Encounter

Altho she amused and confused me some,
I did not wish to portray an arrogant egoism.
(I had seen too much of it in others I encountered).
(I had learned to despise it in myself, so I needed to learn to relate)--
Therefore I tried to be understanding and pleasant,
Not arrogant or reticent.

Remembering her frailty, remembering her mind,
Knowing we (all) are ever-growing, in this moment of time--
All of us are, and all of us should
Remember...... ourselves, if only we would!

More understanding and patience and growing,
All of us could acquire - 'twould help in our knowing!
Old and young alike, we are not yet there,
'til God is done - so be about and be aware--
Remember your encounters and take a care!

Lorna Sparks Gutierrez

Inspiration: People we encounter everyday

Inspirational Verse
Luke 6:31 (NKJV)
"And just as you want men to do to you, you also do to them likewise."

The Little Jewel Box

The Little Jewel Box

The flea market was busy - the sun shown ever so bright!
Mom and I were enjoying a shopping spree in the dream I had last night.

We eyed over items, choosing one or two here and there.
I chose a ruby with silver ring and a little pin-cushion chair.

Mom picked out a cameo brooch and a furry scarf of fox--
Suddenly my hand stumbled upon filigreed handles of a little jewel box!

I guessed it had to be of some value - it appeared quite old.
Surely the delicate sunflowers on the side were worth their weight in gold!

My fingers ran across the beauty of ivory roses atop inlaid.
I'll chance this for a bargain! "How much?" I asked. Fifty cents, I paid!

When we got home, Mom vanished to the kitchen to make us some tea.
"Come here, Mom, and see." I said, laughing heartily!

I sat in my rocking chair, examining more closely what we'd bought.
And, as I showed Mom the jewel box, its elegant loveliness our eyes had caught!

Atop the box, encircled by the roses and a circle of purple hyacinths so wee,
Sat a white lily; and, the box was footed at the bottom by more silver filigree.

Inside, it was lined by golden satin and an oval mirror in its lid.
There was nothing else inside the box - except the love which could not be hid!

Strangely I could feel a spirit of love about the case.
It seemed for someone it had once been precious - a treasure as delicate as lace!

I then could feel that spirit strongly; It seemed to ask of me:
"Would I care for this box as she had?"
(She'd loved it so dearly!)

"Oh, yes!" I responded. In compassion I did feel.
I felt her spirit smile - and then leave, for she knew my answer was real.

Then a strange enlightenment went thru me, I had not known 'er this glimpse!
God had revealed this to me: the treasured box was more than a gift!

For if I in compassion to a spirit unknown, can answer in real, true love--
Can't you believe God cares more for you and me, that He'll answer us from above?*

So dear friend, think about it! Aren't our lives more than a little jewel case?
Let our hearts in compassion be - an answer of love, un-effaced!

Lorna Sparks Gutierrez

Inspirational Verse
Matthew 13:52 (NKJV)
52 Then He said to them, "Therefore every scribe instructed concerning the kingdom of heaven is like a householder who brings out of his treasure things new and old."
*Matthew 7:7-12 has related spiritual meaning: please read these verses.

The Lord Is My Lovely

In precious, quiet moments, Jesus speaks to me,
Alone or in public, wherever we might be.

My Lord that loves me - my only Precious One,
My Beautiful Savior - the Light of my Heart - God's Son!

I'm never alone....He's always here
In my heart to spread happiness and cheer.

In every living moment, we are never apart.
I'll forever remember.....the Savior of my heart.

The Lord is my Anchor, beneath and above me.
For Christ is my Everything....HE is my Lovely!

Lorna Sparks Gutierrez

The Sacred Angels

The Sacred Angels, in my mind I see,
Whose eyes have seen God,
They watch over me.

It amazes me that these Holy Ones have touched God.
And have come down to bless with their
Presence, this earthen sod.

The world would be poor indeed,
If compassion hadn't blessed us to meet our need.
Thank you God for the Angels, Your friends,
Who serve You and love You - without end!

Angels, whose rich stories, you have upon us bestowed:
Amazing spiritual riches – and some of those, foretold.
Angels were with us then, and they are with us now!
God has a good reason for them.
I'm glad He knows why and how!

Lorna Sparks Gutierrez

Thoughts on Actions

The quietest person can speak the loudest just in the things one behooves.
More can be said in the life that is lead, by courses one takes to improve.

By showing one cares, sometimes he must dare, to act in a way 'au contraire'.
One must be brave in order to save, a life of even a knave.

If one wants to be good, he must do as he should, even as he, maybe could.
So remember this, as life is not bliss, in totality of life, all things consist!

One's actions do matter, lest life be in tatters.
Then, one might have to rebuild upon the latter!

Please don't forget, lest you may regret,
To finish those actions undone as yet!

Actions and inactions sum up one's life, making peace or making strife.
Take courage, take hope, as in these actions, they do help one to cope.

And in these thoughts I'm here to say,
Be the best you can in your actions today!

Lorna Sparks Gutierrez

200

There's A Reason

I believe there must be a reason
For all that happens on this earth;
For some acquire great fortune and fame,
And for others it seems a wretched curse!

I say, "There must be a reason!", altho
I can't understand it all or why.
My faith tells me that I'll understand
Someday in that "sweet bye and bye".

Sometimes I believe it must be fate, altho
The Bible implies* that prayer changes things.
And if my faith does not falter,
I'll see the answer prayer brings!

I can't understand the reason for sickness or sin,
Or why there are sorrows on the earth without and within.
But I shall trust the Master - I'll allow Him to lead my hand.
Perchance, then some day we shall all understand--
Upon our joyous entrance to the promised Heavenly Land!

Lorna Sparks Gutierrez

Inspirational Verse
*James: 5:16 (KJV)
........The effectual fervent prayer of a righteous man availeth much!
Also read Romans 8:28

Think About It!

Watch your temper--
Don't lose your head.
Have power o' er your own self,
Or you could end up dead!

Watch that temper--
You'll be glad you did!
Don't listen to the devil,
Or you'll believe a fib!

Keep power o'er your own self.
Be master of your fate.
Get smart - be brilliant,
Before it is too late!

Resist that old devil now!
Get hip - be COOL!
Then you will be wise,
And no one can call YOU a fool!

Lorna Sparks Gutierrez

Inspirational Verses
Proverbs 14:17 (NIV)
A quick-tempered man acts foolishly...
Proverbs17:28 (NIV)
Even fools are thought to be wise if they keep silent - and discerning, if they hold their tongues.
Ecclesiastes 7:9 (NIV)
Be not quickly provoked in your spirit, for anger resides in the lap of fools.
Ecclesiastes 7:17 (NKJV))
Do not be overly wicked, nor be foolish: why should you die before your time?
Ecclesiastes 9:17 (NIV)
The quiet words of the wise are more to be heeded than the shouts of the ruler of fools.
Proverbs 16:32 (NIV)
Better (to be) a patient person than a warrior, one with SELF-CONTROL, than one who takes a city.

To My Teacher
(From A Student)

I'm hoping by this written treat,
Your eyes will smile, as you I greet!
And, may your heart a hug receive,
As you read these words and do believe--

That my teacher makes a difference
In my little life!--
For now I am able to read,
And am able to write!

By your wisdom, the world is a better place;
For, it shows upon the mind and heart
Of each little face!

In your classroom, and
May God bless,
You, at the end of each day,
With peace and rest!

Lorna Sparks Gutierrez

Well Change For The Better

This world is blown by a Godly Wind
To rid us of shame, ignorance, and sin!--

For, we are born into a world that does its best
To express of its depravity, sin, and godlessness!

Of the Good that we know, we must to others teach--
To enlighten a world to Freedom, to others we must reach!

But a friend once told to me a little rhyme,
(That I did stash away in the cache of my mind)--
That "a man convinced against his will,
Was of the same opinion still!" *

SO, should I influence another of what I know,
Only time will tell if any change should show.
The Lord's Work, It, His Spirit will do.
For only He can change a man - and that is true!

Lorna Sparks Gutierrez

Inspirational Verses

Romans 8:16 (NKJV)
"The Spirit Himself bears witness with our spirit that we are children of God."
Proverbs 15:31-33 (NKJV)
"The ear that hears the rebukes of life will abide among the wise. (32) "He who disdains instruction despises his own soul. But he who heeds rebuke gets understanding." (33) "The fear of the Lord is the instruction of wisdom. And before Honor is humility."
Proverbs 22:6 (NKJV)
"Train up a child in the way he should go, and when he is old he will not depart from it."
*Thanks, Kathleen!

Yes or No? Horse Before the Cart!

Today's youth will not listen to wise advice.
They will do things their own way,
Believing 'that' will suffice!--

And then when events take a turn for the worse,
They blame God, even tho, they did not follow
His Advice, His Verse!

They want to do Life their way, and then
They get in a pinch!
And, after you advised them of the possibilities,
Those fears could make any fellow wince!

They heap sorrow upon sorrow upon their own hearts;
For, they did not think to put horses before the carts!

It is so much better to avoid all this shame and this pain,
By taking God's advice and listening to Wisdom's refrain!--

By learning strength of Character and learning Wisdom's care,
By growing and ever learning - by only Wisdom's dare!--

By side-stepping Disobedience and shunning Dishonor's game,
One shall grow and conquer - and be Victor over Blame!

Lorna Sparks Gutierrez

P.S. You want to be your best? Obey God, learn what He wants from you, and His best will assuredly come!

Inspirational Verses
Read Proverbs!
Also: Psalms 37:4-5 and Psalms 37:37 (NKJV)
(4) Delight yourself also in the Lord, and He shall give you the desires of your heart.
(5) Commit your way to the Lord, Trust also in Him, and He shall bring it to pass.
(37) Mark the blameless man, and observe the upright; For the future of that an is PEACE.

This poem is in reference to ANY perspective, and especially the controversy of sex before marriage.

Yet Still, My Journey

A little skinny,.......A little fat--
Been there,.......done that!

A little tired,........A little weak--
Somewhat excited, stronger,.......then chic!

Traveling here,........Traveling there--
An emotional journey to Anywhere!

So where do I want to be? And what do I want to see?
To stand firmly centered - as seen where I'd gone;
Those lessons learned to make me strong!--

Working out my own salvation on this journey Alee--
To leave others better - my mission, a "Fait Accompli"!

Lorna Sparks Gutierrez

Alee (the sheltered side)
Christ is my Shelter, my Alee
"Fait accompli", French for a "fact accomplished"
"Yet still", in hopes that by written words,
these words will help heal hearts after I am gone from my journey!
P.S.
We can only hope we might leave others better off
for them having been there with us. And God forgive
us if we have harmed anyone! Just as we forgive others,
may others forgive us also! Thank You, Lord for forgiving us on our journey to You!
Thank You for traveling with us daily on this journey!

Ye Oil of Forgiveness

Set yourself down in an easy chair,
And set the offense at your feet;
And over the offense you must declare
A statement: _of forgiveness for your own release!_

By your side is an imaginary box,
And inside it, a flask:
Containing the oil of forgiveness,
Spiritually real, to perform that task.

Take that box to sit at your lap,
And uncork that bottle so fair!
And over the offense at your feet,
You must pour out that oil so rare!

"I forgive, I forgive.",
From the heart must be said--
And as you pour, the offense then is dead.
Then re-cork that oil for another to use,
And save the recipe of words you said.

For offenses will come, and offenses will go--.
*And that "oil" – yours – to help you live.
It will help anyone, I must say,
In that act of "I must, I must to forgive!"

Lorna Sparks Gutierrez

Inspirational Verse

Matthew 6:12-15(AKJV)
Jesus' words—
(12) "And forgive us our debts, as we forgive our debtors. (13) And lead us not into temptation, but deliver us from evil; For Thine is the kingdom, and the power, and the glory, forever. Amen. (14) For if ye forgive men their trespasses, your heavenly Father will also forgive you: (15) But if ye forgive not men of their trespasses, neither will your Father forgive your trespasses."
*People in the Bible were anointed with oil. Now we are anointed with the Holy Spirit. Those who have the Holy Spirit MUST forgive others. He is Spiritual, and we need (His) Anointing Oil of His Spirit to live and to forgive others and....ourselves!
The oil of forgiveness is That of the Holy Spirit; The Flask (bottle) that contains It, Is your Heart! Have you opened your heart to The Holy Spirit to allow Him to dwell there? It is my personal belief that the only way you will be able to forgive, is by the Omnipotent Help of the Holy Spirit! In Zechariah 4:6 (AKJV), it says: 'Not by might nor by power, but by My Spirit', saith the Lord of Hosts!

You Who Hung The Stars In Place

* * * * * * *

You who hung the stars in place,
You who make the planets to rotate,
You who formed me in my mother's womb,
You who for us - left us an empty tomb!
You who loved us so much to die for - even me,
To give me life thru out eternity,
Can assuredly hear my small whispered prayer,
To answer us in a right time; for us **all** you do care!
Oh, Lord God who designed all the stars,
Too numerous for me to know--
Oh, Lord God who lives among the stars,
Your glory and celestial majesty,
This gift you do show!

* * * * * * *

Lorna Sparks Gutierrez

Inspiration:
Looking at the morning sky, I saw the planets and stars; I knew then He had that power to answer my lowly prayer!